In Country

MY MEMORIES OF VIETNAM AND AFTER

BY FORREST R. LINDSEY

DORRANCE
PUBLISHING CO
EST. 1920
PITTSBURGH, PENNSYLVANIA 15238

Dorrance Publishing Co
585 Alpha Drive
Pittsburgh, PA 15238
Visit our website at *www.dorrancebookstore.com*

ISBN: 978-1-6393-7166-2
eSIBN: 978-1-6393-7977-4

Dedication

To my family and to all those young men who we lost over there and to their families, forever in our memories.

In Country

MY MEMORIES OF VIETNAM AND AFTER

Introduction

WE STOPPED FOR THE EVENING IN A DESERTED VILLAGE JUST short of where we were going to meet up with the battalion and set up our outposts around us. Almost as soon as it got dark, we heard a burst of very fast submachinegun fire and two Marines in one of our outposts were dead. We had an infiltrator somewhere near us.

I was with the company commander, since I was their artillery scout and because I was only a Lance Corporal, I was put on radio watch, sitting on a concrete porch at the front of a large, deserted house. I had three radios around me: the Company Command net, the Local Security net, and my own artillery Conduct of Fire net. One of my jobs was to check the six outposts every fifteen minutes to make sure that they were awake and alive. I would quietly say: "Golf One, Golf One – this is Golf. If all secure, negative contact, key your handset twice," and the men out there staring into the dark would squeeze the rubber-covered button on their handset twice, making a "Pssht, Psssht" sound on my radio. I would do that for each of the six outposts, one by one in turn.

It was the darkest night I have ever known. You literally couldn't see your hand in front of you, even inches away. It felt like I was totally blind. My uniform was soaked in sweat, and I shivered in the humid dark.

Then, I sensed something directly in front of me and I shoved my M-14 in front of me and pushed the safety off and turned the selector to full auto. I was fully alert and staring as hard as I could in front of me, but it was impossible to see anything, and I couldn't hear any sounds. I waited, my arms holding the rifle shaking, using every sense I had – but nothing. I couldn't just shoot, because there were Marines out there all around me sleeping and I couldn't take the chance of hitting them. I stayed put, intently watching and listening for several minutes until I was sure that it had just been imagination. After several minutes, I put the rifle back on "safe" and put it back across my lap.

Then I heard the loud "Pop" of a .45 and saw a brief flash to my right front. I whispered, "Who shot?" and a voice answered, "Dog Handler" and then, "The dog saw something." I was back to being fully tense again, rigidly pointing my rifle directly forward, safety off.

Dawn came about 4:30 in the morning and I was mad at myself for wasting a night wide awake. I never went to find my relief in the dark because I was so damned scared. I was tired now and I knew that we had the assault about to begin. I got up and walked around to shake off the stiffness and saw dozens of Marines getting up from their night on the ground –.

Then I noticed a man lying on his back, arms and legs outstretched, eyes wide open, wearing only loose black shorts, with a submachinegun on his chest, held by a thick black string around his neck. I walked over to look at him and saw that the top of his head was gone and that the Dog Handler's bullet had hit him in the left temple.

The Dog Handler told me that when the dog silently alerted, he put his hand with the .45 on the dog's head and fired at where the dog was looking.

He was heading directly for me and the sound of my radios, in the dark.

This is the story of my time as a young Marine, serving in Vietnam in the early part of that war and my experiences afterward. Eventually, I advanced further in rank and responsibilities in the Marines and left my identity as smart-aleck young warrior behind. The memories have always stayed with me though, and I wrote these down for my family – and now you – to help provide a context for our war and a time capsule for the views, the cultures, the attitudes of that time in our history. There are a lot of books and movies and other media about the Vietnam War but most of it – in my opinion – don't actually speak to who we really were at that time. The only real claim that I make in this story is that these are the real experiences and memories of a somewhat average guy who watched and listened carefully to what was going on around him and I am preserving it for future generations to read and evaluate on their own.

This book also discusses my view of the reasons for the Vietnam War which I have gleaned at the time and the years after, but generally without the benefit of any help from our government. It almost seems as though we were expected to go and fight and hopefully survive but telling us why it was happening hadn't been fully worked out yet. I ended up being fully committed to winning, even if it meant that I lost my life in the process, but it wasn't thanks to any pep talks from the leadership of our country at the time. If anything, it seemed as though our leaders considered us to be an annoying afterthought to whatever they were working on.

Wars are terrible, life-changing things. Yet when there is a war, some young men line up and prepare to do their duty. Some do it because their fathers did. Some do it for the adventure, going places that they haven't been, experiencing new things, maybe proving themselves as men. Others join because they are forced to, and yet more join because they have nothing much to live for.

I was one of those "all of above" cases.

I remember who we were, and I know that, even given the benefit of hindsight, I would have volunteered - even knowing what I know now about our war. I would be drawn back by that long line of friends, young men who I knew and trusted, carrying my rifle, warily watching the tree lines and rows of gravestones for any movement, any shadow that told me that my enemies were there, waiting for us.

This is my story, my own history and my memories only. Every single person who experienced the Vietnam War has his own unique perspective and different memories of it. That's because the war was different for the different services, the different jobs, the different views, different locations, different periods of the war, different mindsets, and even just being a little way away from each other. I can't claim to have a better perspective or a more correct view, but I was very observant back then and for whatever reason, I still have very clear memories of nearly everything. I have to also mention that these are the memories of a 19-21-year-old Lance Corporal and reflect my knowledge and attitudes of that time. Later on, once I'd grown up a bit more and had greater experience and responsibilities, I came to see things in more context and with some more wisdom, but I am still proud of that kid that I used to be. That said, as you'll see when you read my story, you'll understand why I learned to watch out for characters like me, as I advanced further in the Marine Corps.

According to my service history in Vietnam, I was part of 19 operations:

Wyoming, Oregon, Virginia, Cherokee, Hastings, Prairie, Troy, Cannon, Teton, Kern, Shasta, Mississippi, Shasta II, Stone, Lafayette, Early, Canyon, Yell, Union.

But for the most part, everything blended together, and I really don't remember even being informed at the time which operation started and which operation ended or even what they were called at the time. Just makes an interesting and almost meaningless list for my record book. I was part of the early period of the Vietnam War when we were just getting started with major US combat operations; my viewpoint was relatively untouched by the propaganda that was evolving at home, and we were still learning about the enemy and developing our responses to them as they were developing their responses to us.

When we look back this half century to our war in Vietnam, the usual attitude is that it was a "waste" and a "nightmare" and the soldiers who fought there are looked upon as unwilling and hapless and even prone to criminal atrocities. Those people who "rose in opposition" to the Vietnam War are depicted as "young people of conscience" who picked the right side, heroes of a necessary resistance – at least that's what you find in most of the histories we are provided.

The truth is different. The Vietnam War was slowly and inexorably pushed on our country as the latest stratagem of the Cold War. The Soviets and their allies in the Warsaw Pact saw Southeast Asia as the perfect place to expand their global power and after years of careful support and planning, aided their acolyte, Ho Chi Minh, in his drive to seize all of Vietnam to be under his brand of communism. This new direction for communist expansion was called the "National Liberation War" and it was the strategy of sponsoring, training, and supporting an internal civil war to guide it to their ends. In this case, it was to gain control of post-colonial Asia, gain sea control using Vietnamese ports to strangle US support of Asian allies, surround a hostile communist China with pro-Soviet states, and once again, show the US to be too faint-hearted and "decadent" to resist them: a "Paper Tiger."

In the years before the major US entry into Vietnam in 1965, the American media depicted the struggle in Vietnam as a series of atrocities committed by the communist Vietcong. *Life, Collier's,* and the *Saturday Evening Post* magazines, among others, had several series of illustrated articles showing the effects of the VC terror campaign of bombing of civilian meeting places, assassinations, and taking over the villagers' food supplies. As the US sent in advisors in the early '60s, stories and features of their suffering and heroism were standard fare.

One of those articles in *Life Magazine* in May 1965, featured a Marine Helicopter Crew Chief experiencing the loss of another helicopter and the death of his friend at the hands of VC in a series of excellent and moving photographs. I read that magazine when it came out and resolved to join him in that fight. My thought was "I'm not better than he is."

In those days, that wasn't that unusual for a young man: Our parents served during WWII (and some grandparents during WWI), so service in the Armed Forces was considered a first step in our citizenship and a required male rite of passage. We had a war on, and it was "our turn." I knew a little more than most since I read a great deal and I had read all of Bernard Fall's books about the French war in Indochina and I was also a little bit older than most enlistees at almost 20 years old.

Table of Contents

Joining The Marines

I WAS NOT AN IDEAL TYPE TO JOIN THE MARINES. I AM NEARSIGHTED and wore glasses. I was skinny. I was not athletic and while I was in high school, I was the favorite target for bullies-in-training to try to beat up after school. The Marine Corps didn't care – I was above room temperature, stood upright, and had all my limbs and they would take care of the rest. I am sure that most of you have had more than enough Marine Boot Camp stories, so I won't expand much on it except that it was everything you have heard about and worse. We were shaved bald, screamed at in the foulest possible terms 24/7, run for miles, pushed over obstacles, punched, and threatened and drilled for long hours in the heat. After 13 weeks, the impossible happened and I was abruptly a Marine. I had gained muscle, confidence, a huge vocabulary of filthy words and phrases, some barroom fighting skills, and the feeling that I could "kick a__ and take names," whether it was true or not.

We all went on to an Infantry Training Regiment (ITR) at Camp Pendleton a little farther up the California coast, which was much less like Boot Camp, but rigorous as we went on long full-equipment hikes, fired several kinds of weapons from rifles (which were the venerable M1 Garands from WWII and Korea – the Marine Corps had tons of surplus ammunition for them) to machine guns and flamethrowers to learn combat skills. The main feature that I remember from ITR was the Crawling Circles: we learned the specialty of crawling, butt down, flat as possible to the ground, inching our way forward, round and round those gravel circles until my buttons wore off my utilities. Our "commencement exercise" was to crawl under live machine gun fire, fired 18 inches above the ground by two .30 caliber machine guns while we crawled under barbed wire entanglements and while they set off quarter pound blocks of TNT in sandbagged holes among us. Guess that was what all the crawling was about. After our four weeks there, we were sent to our Military Occupational Specialty (MOS) schools for another four weeks. In my case, the Marine Corps looked me over, studied my test results, considered my one year of college education and then sent me to Motor Transport School to learn how to drive a 5-Ton truck.

Truck Driving School was a pleasant break in the so far frenetic training routine. All it involved was learning the working parts of the M54 5-Ton truck and driving all over the hills of Camp Pendleton. I was not an enthusiastic truck driver because almost all of my prior driving experience was motorcycles and the size, lack of visibility, and multiple levers for the complex transmission made me dislike driving them. I passed anyway. One of the incidents I remember during the training was night driving. We were trained to watch the really dim red "tactical" ("Cat's Eyes") rear lights of the trucks when following another truck. That evening it was raining lightly as we were convoying along dirt roads in the hills paralleling the Pacific Ocean. Per our training, if you saw two dim red lights, one per side, you were at the right distance. If you saw four of those small lights, you were way too close and needed to back off. As we were slowly moving down the road, I suddenly lost sight of any lights and stopped the truck completely. This caused my instructor to get excited until we got out and discovered that the trucks just ahead of me had driven off a small embankment and were lying on their sides to the left below us.

The next and last stop was Staging Battalion in another part of Camp Pendleton (14 Area) where we were trained specifically for deployment for war. We did squad and platoon attack and defense exercises, learned more about Vietnam specifically, learned about recognizing and avoiding mines and booby traps including a well-designed course that forced us to navigate down trails with tripwires attached to small but very loud charges. We patrolled through simulated Vietnamese villages. We were shown graphic combat medic movies for training us on how to deal with wounds, using real combat casualty footage. It was very sobering to see for the first time, real wounds and shocked-looking young men, bleeding their lives out.

We also learned about the Marine Corps' penchant for goofy humor: in one demonstration of the "firepower of the Marine Rifle Squad," we watched thirteen men in a trench in front of our bleachers fire at an intense rate for about a minute, expending hundreds, maybe even thousands of rounds. It was a heart-pounding sight and sound, but nobody thought that maybe the "firepower of the Vietcong Rifle Squad" made exactly the same intense racket but in OUR direction.

Just as the echoes of that thunderous display stopped, our commentator – a tall, barrel chested Staff Sergeant – told us that "Marine Corps development had designed a new rifle round that would replace the firepower of the squad": he held the round of ammunition with green and white rings around its nose high in the air for all of us to see; then he placed it into his rifle, took aim and fired. There was a slight pause as the bullet raced downrange and then a huge, shocking explosion about 500 meters from us. He turned to us and said: "Gentlemen, I present the 7.62mm NUCLEAR round!" At that point in my development as a Marine, I think I believed him and looked forward to using those things.

At Staging Battalion, we lived in wooden WWII barracks, and we were housed in what was known as an "open squad bay"; it was wide open from one entrance to the opposite side, and we had bunkbeds in rows on either side and the common "head" (the bathroom) was down a hall. Some nights we'd have what I called the "Battle of the Bands," where some Marines would put one type of music (Soul or Rock) on their record players and some others would set up their record players to play Country. Each side would elevate the volume until the barracks was filled with an awful, combined racket and then the fistfights would begin. Usually, nobody was too badly hurt – those days, fistfights ended when your adversary fell down or just said "enough" and the fights were one on one, not several against one. Usually, the fighters of the night before were friends by morning. Beer played a large role in those fights.

During my stay in Staging Battalion, I also had to serve on the Regimental Guard, guarding ammunition dumps and the like for long hours in our dress green uniforms with cartridge belts and M-14 rifle and ten rounds of ammunition. On early Christmas morning, I saw the very first snowfall of my life (I'm from Southern California) at an ammunition dump in the hills and I scraped up a little snow to make my first snowball. I put it on the ground and using my rifle as a golf club, whacked it. Just that moment a large black car arrived at my post and a General came out of the car and fixed me with a hard look after I saluted, and he asked what I was doing. I said: "golf, Sir?" and he said, "Merry Christmas, A__hole"; got back into his car and left.

Late one evening those of us on regimental guard were called out and issued bandoleers of live ammunition. We were told that there had been a riot at the base brig (prison) and that we were being sent to end it. When we arrived at the brig, we were told to load our rifles and fix bayonets and that if we met any resistance when we entered the brig, we were to shoot to kill. When we went in the entrance of the brig, there was blood and broken glass all over but everyone we saw were in their beds and "sleeping," so we didn't have to shoot anyone.

A memorable feature of Staging Battalion were the many inoculations we had to have before leaving for Vietnam. In one day, we received a total of 30 shots each, one corpsman at each shoulder, firing compressed air inoculation guns in a long line. When we were back out in the daylight and standing in formation, I saw the man at the far end of our file fall forward flat on his face on the concrete. Then the next guy fell exactly the same way, then next, until I fell on my face too. I woke in my squad bay bunk to the welcome news that the afternoon run had been cancelled for us. Bad lot of Gamma Globulin, apparently.

I went home to my family in Sepulveda, California, for a short leave before deploying to Vietnam and I remember my father driving, just him and me, in the family station wagon back to Camp Pendleton in early January 1966. My Dad and I hadn't been very close while I was growing up, so it was strange and comforting at the same time. I was going to war, so whatever differences we had had before were left behind.

I joined a group of about 30 other Marines who I didn't know, and we went by bus to an Air Force base to get on a plane. I heard one of the Marines tell another that he knew "how to get out of going to Vietnam," that all he had to do was go over to a Major that was sitting nearby and kiss him (homosexuality being an immediate Undesirable Discharge in those days). The Marine he was telling this said: "well, how do you know he (the Major) won't like it?" After a moment's reflection, he decided not to go forward with his plan.

Marines waiting to ship out to Vietnam at Staging Battalion, Camp Pendleton, California (Photo by Ramon R. Alba, used with permission)

January 16, 1966, we were all packed into a KC-135 tanker (an Air Force Boeing 707) aircraft that was temporarily converted for passengers. It had nylon web seats and it stank of jet fuel and the only in-flight meals we had were cold sandwiches and then C-Rations (canned meals, usually dating from 1942). "Nothing but the best for our boys in green.." We landed in Hawaii at Hickam Field and spent one evening watching Honolulu in the distance – no liberty for us, of course – just fistfighting and being bitten by hundreds of mosquitos. In the morning, we ate breakfast at an excellent Air Force mess hall (I left a complimentary note and quarter tip) before launching again for Okinawa.

We landed at night in a storm at Kadena Air Force Base – the aircraft swerved a bit on landing in the strong winds – and we were bused to a barracks where we would stay for two days. Our bus driver was an angry looking older white civilian with some sort of long fleshy tumors hanging from the bottom of his ears, like fat icicles. It was hard to take your eyes off those things. They wiggled disgustingly every time he moved his head. When were setup in the barracks, we were told to turn in all of our dress and noncombat uniforms in our seabags for storage there in Okinawa. Supposedly we were to get them back at the end of our tour in Vietnam, but the feeling seemed to be that it was the last time we'd see them again. In the evenings, we were besieged in our barracks by American civilian salesmen, selling us life insurance policies, ornate Bibles, and expensive watches on credit. It struck me as bizarre that the US government would let those vultures near us, to try to take what little money we had as they took advantage of our fears.

Arrival

SOON ENOUGH, WE RE-BOARDED OUR TRUSTY JET TANKER AND flew to Danang. When the jet stopped and the door opened, we were hit in the face with a blast of humid heat and the stink of s__t. Welcome to Vietnam. My first view was of a row of freshly-built wood buildings with corrugated sheet steel roofs, with the sun glaring off them. We were marched to a building accompanied by the constant roar of jet aircraft on full afterburner, drowning every other sound out, a numbing noise that overwhelmed your senses. Three of us new arrivals were driven to another set of buildings and a young and friendly lieutenant sat us on the steps of the building and asked us where we wanted to go: Chu Lai, Danang, or Phu Bai. Obviously, none of us had any idea what distinguished these locations from another, but I picked Phu Bai, since I had never heard of it before. The lieutenant initialed my orders and told me to walk down the hill to the airfield to hitch a ride on one of the helicopters going to Phu Bai. I was almost to the helicopters when a gunnery sergeant stopped me, handed me a rifle and told me to watch a group of about twenty prisoners that were sitting on the ground in a group – all blindfolded and with their arms tied behind them. The gunny told me to stop them if they try to talk to each other and to shoot them if they caused trouble. I wasn't sure at that point that I was ready to shoot anyone but as soon as the gunny left, one of the older prisoners with a short wispy beard began to whisper to the man next to him. I was sure that English wouldn't work, so I used some high school French: *"Taisez-vous, - ou Je casse vôtre tête"* which I was sure meant "shut up or I (will) break your head." Whatever I said, it worked; they stopped trying to talk to each other and I didn't have to shoot any of them.

After the gunny returned, I gave him his rifle back and walked to a group of Sikorsky UH-34 helicopters that were thunderously warming up and I yelled to the crew chief – "Phu Bai?" and he nodded, and I got aboard for the short flight north. Phu Bai, it turned out, was about eight miles south of Hue City on the main paved north-south coastal highway of Vietnam, Highway 1. There was a good-sized airfield there, a field hospital (Alpha Company, 3rd Medical Battalion), the army 8th Radio Relay Unit (actually an electronic intelligence unit despite the innocuous name) and one artillery battery.

That 105mm artillery battery emplaced there was, according to my orders, my home: Battery B, 1st Battalion, 11th Marines. At first, I was assigned to be the driver for a 155mm howitzer that was temporarily assigned to Bravo. They were very unhappy to discover that my truck driver's training hadn't included learning how to back up with a towed load. I did tow that beast around anyway for a while, but when it was time to back the thing up into its firing position, the Section Chief – an older and sour Staff Sergeant – would make some incomprehensible hand signals until I jackknifed the howitzer and had to start all over again. The battery would fire often from its position in Phu Bai towards the West in support of some infantry battalion out that way, all day and sometimes into the night. When I wasn't actually driving, I was required to help clean and fire that gun, a 155mm M114 howitzer. The M114 was an old WWII weapon that fired a 96-pound projectile (shell) and was loaded from the rear by opening the breech, two men pushing the shell into the chamber with an aluminum ramming staff, and then another Marine would push in the correct number of white bags of powder. The breech would be slammed shut; then a small brass cartridge the size of a .38 Special pistol cartridge but without a bullet would be enclosed in a small aperture at the back of the breech block, and then a short rope with a wood knob at the far end (a lanyard) was attached to a firing lever. If the howitzer was all aligned and ready, the Gunner would yank on that lanyard and that short-barreled monster would roar and flood the area with concussion and poisonous-smelling and choking gas, filling your eyes with tears. Bad as it was, I suspect it was a lot worse at the enemy end of things. When it was time to move the thing to a new position and set it up, my job, as the least worthwhile member of the gun crew, was to stand with one other less worthy Marine at the front of the gun and push and pull at a 3-foot steel rod that slowly jacked the whole gun into the air on its firing platform, clearing the huge tires from touching the ground. It was a lot of hard work just to move that thing up even a few inches because it weighed 12,800 pounds and we were lifting every bit of it, stroke by sweaty stroke.

I hated that thing.

When I wasn't actively towing or firing that howitzer, I was assigned to the battery motor pool where most of the drivers and mechanics and all of the trucks stayed when they weren't actually on the road. Even though we were "in combat," it was laid out in peacetime precision with exactly lined up trucks in rows and a fairly comfortable wood-framed and floored tent as our home within the battery. It was clean and relatively neat, and we had some room for our cots and personal items. The routine wasn't very difficult or dangerous at that point and the most demanding thing we had as part of being in that motor pool was standing two hours every few nights as the guard. The guard duty seemed a bit stupid: we had our own perimeter, complete with barbed wire and machine gun posts around the whole battery. Then we had an infantry battalion and the airfield and their security perimeters. Bored and tired, it seemed completely pointless as you walked those two hours in big circles around the lines of trucks and our tent. Until one night in a heavy fog, when another guard and I spotted four people walking through our area, carrying a pole between two of them. We called for them to halt and the Vietcong mortar team that had blundered into the middle of all of our security rings quietly surrendered. I got my very first "war souvenir," a long hooked "bamboo knife" that one of the VC had been carrying.

The Author in his Motor Transport tent and the souvenir "Bamboo Knife". Note the M-14 Rifle and the packs with rifle ammunition and a grenade hanging from it. Note too, the battery-powered record player next to my cot. Such was technology at that time. (Photo from the Author's Collection)

At this point in my story, I will describe Vietnam as we saw it then: where we were. It was rice paddies, rivers and clusters of small villages in heavy vegetation we called "tree lines." About half the time or more, the rice paddies were flooded with ankle to knee deep water framed by earth dikes in rectangular patterns. Water buffalos grazed out in the paddies and fields and kids played out with them as they tended them. In the tree lines, the houses and buildings of the villagers were scattered among them, as the families that lived in them grew their crops and lived their lives. If the village was prosperous, there would be a Buddhist temple or even a Catholic church among them and one or more wells. The houses themselves were for the most part made of thatch with one or two houses made of wood or block that belonged to someone with more money. Each home had a banana grove and sometimes mango or papaya or other fruit trees, and within each of these homes was a centrally located "family bunker" for the family to seek cover when the war arrived at their homes. There were small markets that sold fruit or vegetables or goods in the large village clusters (Vietnamese villages were often scattered over a fairly large area and numbered, such as "Cam Ne 1, Cam Ne 2, Cam Ne 3," etc.).

In the far distance away from the coast there were tall, dark mountains dense with jungle that was home to the elephant, the tiger, and of course, our enemy. While I was there, we fought primarily among the villages but sometimes ventured into the mountains to fight. But where we were, there were more than enough of the enemy to keep us busy.

Our battery would frequently pack up and deploy to positions farther to the west and north to support operations farther away. During one of these deployments, we fired our required missions and packed up to go back to Phu Bai but my truck, still towing that miserable M114 howitzer suddenly lost power and began to slow down, way down. The rest of our battery convoy kept going and we barely chugged along at four or five miles an hour. We stopped to check out the engine – with that same angry Section Chief glaring and yelling – but none of us had any idea of what was causing the engine to drag. We got going again, mindful of the danger we were facing as a single truck and cannon, crawling down an open road and loaded with high explosive ammunition, alone to the enemy. As we creeped along, I remember seeing several young Vietnamese women skinny dipping in a river and waving at us happily. Somehow even that sight didn't distract us much from the feeling that we would be blown to Hell any second. A small Cessna-sized observation plane showed up over us and flew in circles around our slow procession until we finally reached friendly territory. It turned out that the truck's governor – a device to limit the truck's top speed – was malfunctioning and kept our truck at its sluggish and dangerous crawl.

Life in the battery at Phu Bai was more or less routine. The battery had been in that position for a couple of months, so we had a decent tent mess hall for hot meals twice a day, reasonably clean areas to work and other than that hapless VC mortar team, no sign of any enemies. The drivers in the motor pool had their own routines going which included hazing and threatening us new guys, sneaking out of the position at night along a railway line to visit the whorehouses in Hue City, and in one case at least, had a black market operation going. One of the outcasts from the motor pool hierarchy was a guy from New York named PFC C. C and I got along because he hated guard and for a minor stipend, I would take his place and do the extra two hours. One morning, as a reward, he had me drive a run for the mess hall and we headed north up Highway 1 to pick up fresh bread from the Task Force bakery. Except our first turn was to the headquarters of the local Vietnamese army unit and he directed me to park behind their main building. He came out of the building with a big sack full of little sandwiches with some sort of meat in them and a case of Jim Beam whiskey and a pistol wrapped in an oily rag. He paid a Vietnamese soldier with a wad of dollars and then we were on to our next stop. He appeared to double his money at every stop we made – but even though I liked and admired his enterprising spirit, that was the last run I made with him for fear of a court martial. It turned out that the battery leadership was somewhat aware of his dealings but since he could also acquire barbed wire coils, sheets of plywood and unfilled sandbags that somehow couldn't be provided by the supply section, he was left untouched.

As far as I saw, we never received any briefings about the current situation, or discussion of "lessons learned" or even a pep talk. We were just Marines as far as our platoon, battery and battalion level leaders were concerned. Like mushrooms: kept in the dark and fed bulls__t – except even the bulls__t was in short supply. Later, when I joined the infantry, I met a different version of leadership.

We Marines of the 1960s had our own sardonic take on things. The Marine Corps was known as "the Crotch," "the Suck" and the "Green Weenie." Our attitude was reflected in some of our sayings like "One Good Deal after Another" when referring to the Corps and "it figures" was said whenever the leadership asked for something else that seemed stupid or pointless to us. Other sardonic sayings were: "harassment, to be effective, must be continuous" and "Eat the apple and f__k the Corps" and "Every day is a holiday and every meal is a feast – and every payday is a big f__king joke."

We also had funny little ditties we sang like:

> "Oh… the Marine Corps flag is a dirty old rag and the Commandant is a fairy…"

And

> "Jingle bells, Mortar shells, VC in the grass
> If you think we'll be home by Christmas,
> you can kiss my a__"

Even though all of this seems as though a riot was about to start at any minute, it was really just a funny way for us to deal with our role as the bottom end of an autocratic organization. We were fully committed to do our job as told but we didn't have to pretend that we enjoyed it.

As most accounts of the Vietnam War mention, we all kept an individual and current tally of the days remaining for our time left in Vietnam of our 13-month tours. (One of those idiosyncrasies of being a Marine was that we had 13-month tours in Vietnam while the army had 12 months tours. No clue at all why the difference existed; other than one more chance for our leadership to screw with us.) Everyone kept precise track of how many days they had left to go back home and if someone asked, you'd say: "I have one hundred twenty-six days and a wakeup." When you got past the halfway point, say 7 months or so "in country," you'd become a "short timer." As the end date your tour approached, say, within 99 days, you became a "two-digit midget" and you'd use sayings like—"I'm so short, I can sit on a dime and dangle my legs." For the Marines in the rear areas, it was just funny but for the Marines in the infantry, the two most dangerous times were when you were brand new (for obvious reasons) and when you were "short": the superstition, or at least what we thought was superstition, was that people who were almost ready to rotate home were most likely to be killed; usually because of some new guy's mistake.

The people who wanted to stay in the Marine Corps were known as "Lifers" and the last thing anyone wanted to be known as, was a Lifer. Every other word was "f__k": it was a verb, a noun, an adjective, and adverb and it was interjected into every part of our speech. Besides that, there were many other allusions to gay sex by the Staff NCOs, such as: "if I catch you doing that. I'll f__k you right in the a__" and unauthorized hats, like the ones the kids sold us were called "Catch me, f__k me" hats. To my Catholic School mind, it was shocking at first but after a while it blended into numbing meaninglessness because of the incessant use.

My fellow Marines were a bit of a mixed bag. We were all volunteers, a fact that was rubbed in fairly often by our superiors ("I don't want to hear you bitching: you volunteered, you got nobody to blame but yourselves"). In the motor pool, in the firing platoons, among the communicators, we had a pretty wide mix of American middle- and lower-class males. Some were brilliant, some were flat stupid. Some were former criminals, forced by courts to either enlist in the Corps or go to prison. Some of these made good Marines but some also bullied the rest of us and looked for trouble. One guy, PFC K, worked out with homemade weights and pushed everyone around, looking for a fight. I was still skinny and quiet, so I was a main target of K's taunting and shoving but I refused to fight him. During one of my turns at guard, I saw with fear that K was my relief and that I had to wake him for the next watch. I went up to his cot in the tent and tried to wake him by saying his name, no luck. Then I tried shaking his shoulder and he exploded in wild punches, one just grazing my nose. Instinctively, I swung my rifle down, steel buttplate-first into his face. It hurt him badly enough that we had to carry him to the sickbay tent, and I had to stand his two-hour guard for him. I dreaded what would happen the next day but from then on, K was extremely and ostentatiously friendly and kept a good distance from me. I think he thought that I was insane and had hit him with premeditation. After all, everybody has to sleep sometime. I think that that accident worked to my advantage and the thugs kept their distance.

Nothing like crazy to keep people at bay.

From what I could see, very few Marines were at all interested in discussing anything about the history of Vietnam, or ways to improve things tactically, or really anything related to where we were. They discussed sports or music or sex or maybe the new cars coming out but very few had any interest beyond just getting their individual job done and getting home at the end of their 13 months. We got along pretty well, most of us, with the occasional fistfight. I was made fun of because I was interested in history and Vietnam and the weapons and equipment of the enemy. Many of my fellow Marines weren't big thinkers and they were contemptuous of anyone who tried to discuss anything out of a limited number of topics – or with a vocabulary that used words longer than two syllables.

Racial differences were there – it was the mid-'60s – but they evaporated most of the time because we were all in the same boat and worked together and slept in the same tent. After a certain point, despite our differences in background, education, religion, and pretty well everything else, we melded into a more-or-less cohesive family—living together with the same risks, the same heat and sticky humidity, the same insects and rodents and reptiles, and our girlfriends or wives all dumped us at nearly the same time.

Kids watching us in our truck and waiting to mooch some cigarettes. (Photo by Ramon R. Alba, used with permission)

My impressions of Vietnam and its people at the time were simple: the Vietnamese were small, skinny, dark brown people with ramshackle homes, a primitive lifestyle and Vietnam itself was a land of rivers, rice paddies and dark and sullen mountains. We did not have any occasion to try to speak to any Vietnamese person (other than my pidgin French to those prisoners) and our battery and camp allowed no Vietnamese at all to enter. I did finally meet Vietnamese people about a month in for me when, as a "new guy" and expendable, I was given up for temporary duty as a Military Policemen (MP) to man a roadblock to guard the southern entry of Highway 1 into Phu Bai. One other Marine and I were placed next to a village and given the job of stopping all traffic on Highway 1 and "checking identification cards." I put that in quotes because neither of us could speak or read Vietnamese and "checking identification cards" meant staring blankly at a card and pretending that we knew whether it was OK or not. We were given a huge .50 caliber machine gun to enforce our blocking position, but it too was bluff: neither one of us knew how to load or fire it. It was just a menacing piece of decoration. When things got boring, which was most of the time, one of us would visit the Vietnamese village alongside our post just to see what went on.

It was a very poor village and the people there only seemed to have one set of clothes and the kids were naked. Their reaction to us was either friendly or indifferent and after a couple of visits I found an older woman who spoke French and we were able to talk. She told me about their families and their life as farmers and she shared some of her bread with us while we gave her some of our C-Rations. She seemed bemused by us as sort of large, ugly and well-armed children, which was a reasonably accurate description. She told me that they were afraid of the Vietcong, and I could tell that she wasn't just saying it to impress us. I came away feeling more impressed with the Vietnamese warmth and generosity and the overall effect was to convince me that they were good people and that we really were needed there to help protect these people.

Our MP duties were amusing. We would stop some small French-made bus overloaded with too many people – some actually hanging on the outside because there wasn't any room left inside – with huge stacks of sacks and bicycles and baskets piled on top. We would signal them to stop, and we would tell everyone to get off and show us their ID. We would go through that charade patiently and politely and almost every time, we'd finish looking and send them on their way north. But one time, an older man got off the bus and ran. We had no trouble at all catching him – he was grey-haired and probably at least 50 years old – and he meekly surrendered when we caught him. He had an ancient Smith and Wesson .38 pistol on him, and he had 20,000 units of penicillin on him that was labeled as a "gift from the American Friends Society (Quakers)." He was a VC doctor, and we took him gently in to the MP station for interrogation – he was quiet and hadn't put up any real resistance. My fellow MP and I returned to our post and played with the VC's .38 by shooting it at a telephone pole, but the old thing was so weak that the bullets only stuck halfway into the pole. He had also had a motorized bicycle, with the motor on top of the front wheel that had been offloaded from that bus. I decided to try it out, so I slung my rifle across my back and pushed that bike until the motor started and rode south down Highway 1. I remember how great the wind felt as I sped down the road, helmet bouncing, flak jacket filling like a sail and then I realized that I was getting farther and farther away from any friendly-controlled areas all on my own and so I turned around and headed back. I'm sure this story would have ended at this point if I had kept riding farther.

My last act in the MP duty was to try to catch an escaped North Vietnamese sergeant prisoner who had gotten away from Alpha Med where he was being treated for his wounds. He was easy to find: he had a large cast over his body and one leg and he was crawling, face down, right out in the open, next to the runway at Phu Bai airfield. I walked next to him for a little bit as he struggled to "escape" and then we picked him up and put him into a jeep to take him back to the hospital. I was impressed with that guy's ferocious determination.

Vietnam was absolutely loaded with kids – thousands and thousands of them. They were everywhere. They were along the roads, out in the fields tending their Water Buffalos, hanging around at the dumps to dig through the trash. Everywhere we went, we saw hundreds at a time, smiling happily at us and mooching anything they could get. We learned a form of pidgin Vietnamese-French-English from them and if we were generous with cigarettes or candy or maybe an extra hat or something we were "number one" and if we didn't give them what they wanted, we were "number ten" or worse, "number ten thousand." "Dinky dau" meant crazy in the head, or something like that and very crazy was "Beaucoup dinky dau." All those cheerful and apparently happy-to-see-us kids were the best part of being there, because they seemed to enjoy our company and our few treasures so much. Somewhere around this time, I was tasked to drive a jeep and trailer to a local orphanage run by a Catholic church and carry several cases of C-Rations to help with their food requirements. When we arrived, we were greeted enthusiastically by a big crowd of kids, and we offloaded the C-Rations while trying to answer all of questions the kids had. They were distracting us – while we were occupied with their chatter, my jeep started up and drove away, with no visible driver. I tried chasing it down the road, but it left me in the dust. After about ten minutes, the jeep returned – and two small kids – one pushing the clutch, brake and accelerator with his hands and the other one standing on the seat and operating the steering wheel. While they did an amazing job of driving, I was annoyed to have my jeep stolen from me – but I got over it quickly enough when I realized that they were just having fun.

This first month and a half was almost routine for us. The guys who had been there a couple of months earlier insisted that things had "been rougher" earlier during their arrival during the previous summer but not really. At that point in the war, the enemy was still sizing us up and working on developing their methods to deal with us. Everything was quiet and ordinary – and a portion of our motor transport section personnel had VD from their covert runs to the cat houses of Hue City. The countryside was beautiful, all shades of green with wide rice fields, with the blue of the sky reflected on the water's surface. At night, the mountains in the distance flashed with lightning almost every evening.

(Photo by Ramon R. Alba, used with permission)

FOOD

When I joined Bravo Battery at Phu Bai we had an established wood-reinforced tent mess hall with wood flooring and similar serving areas and we got two hot meals a day, breakfast and dinner. The food was pretty good, but mostly from large cans, served with meat that had been frozen or also came from cans. We had long wood mess tables like long picnic tables and millions upon millions of flies. The flies covered the tables and when you sat down with your tray, the flies would take off into the air in front of you in a large dirty cloud and then quickly settle on your food if you didn't energetically wave them off with one arm while eating with the other. It should come as no surprise that diarrhea was almost always a problem.

The other meals were C-Rations. Those were canned meals of World War Two vintage which contained a couple of green-painted cans, an accessory pack with chewing gum, matches, salt and pepper packs, an insultingly small pack of toilet paper, and a tiny pack of five cigarettes, often Lucky Strike Green label brand – the pack was colored green instead of red for the duration of the war – (WWII). There was also a thin foil-wrapped disc of tropical chocolate ("S__t Discs") in each box but these were despised because they were gritty-tasting and had an odd chemical smell. Another can contained the crackers that we called "John Wayne" crackers and these we ate with the cheese or peanut butter from yet more small cans. We were hungry, so we ate them, but I sincerely doubt that anyone misses eating those things. Interestingly, we also called the small folding can opener that came with the C-Rations a "John Wayne" but the army called it a "P-38."

The C-Rations themselves had a numbing uniformity and the choices were limited to:

- Beans and Meatballs ("Beans and Balls")
- Bean and Weenies (a favorite)
- Beef and Potatoes ("Beef and Rocks")
- Ham, Sliced
- Turkey Loaf
- Eggs, Chopped
- And of course, the most hideous of them all, Ham and Lima Beans ("Ham and M___f___ers") Normally, Ham and Limas would have been great, but the manufacturer used cuts of ham that came from some disgusting position on a pig (presumably) and was loaded with a foul-smelling grease. The only way to make them even slightly palatable was to drain the can of all fluid, then replace it with water, heat it, then pour out the water. Nobody wanted Ham and Mothers.

There were other items that were included that were sought after, like canned peaches or fruit cocktail or canned bread but the can of fruitcake was another item we avoided. In rear areas, whole cases of C-Rations were opened and only the preferred items taken, and the rest thrown out. The process was known as "Rat F__king" the C-Rations.

We used to heat our C-Rats by punching holes in one of the smaller cans to make it into a little stove and then burned a white, waxy Trioxane fuel tablet in it which was quite capable of heating one or more of the large cans, but it was also capable of choking you like poison gas if you were dumb enough to burn the things in an enclosed space. Later, we also learned that we could heat C-Rations using bits of C-4 explosive which burned hot but safely or pellets of cannon propellant. Those last items required very careful feeding, one at a time, into the fire because they would flare up into a very large and hot flame suddenly and burning yourself was common. It really boiled water fast, though. While I was a truck driver, the other drivers showed me the trick of heating a C-Ration can on the exhaust manifold of my truck: you punched a small hole in the top of the can – for obvious reasons – and then opened the right fold-down section of the engine compartment to put the can on top of the exhaust manifold. About ten minutes of driving and voilà, chow is served. Of course, you had to stop the truck to go get the can from under the hood first. If you were one of the less scientifically adept and didn't punch the holes in the top of the can, you'd have to scrape a whole lot of beans sprayed all over the inside of the engine compartment and put up with that burnt bean smell for a while.

(Photo by Ramon R. Alba, used with permission)

BUGS

There are a number of things about Vietnam that were very alien to most of us, particularly those of us who came from cities and one of the big ones was the flying and crawling critters. I have mentioned the huge clouds of flies around us a lot of the time, but I haven't said anything about that damn biting flies that seemed to have an attraction for elbows. Wherever you were, they would bite you hard enough on the arms and elbows that you'd have a sore patch there and eventually it would make a small, circular scar to remember them by. Mosquitos were everywhere too, mainly at night and the mosquito repellent they gave us might have worked a little, but it had its own drawbacks because it was oily and nasty smelling and would stain your clothes. Many of those mosquitos carried Malaria and other diseases and despite taking huge pills regularly, I caught malaria and so did most everyone else eventually. At night, the really creepy bugs came out and if there was any small amount of light, the bugs would come towards it and you. One we called the "Flying Neck Biter" was about an inch and a half long and had two large claws that covered its head, and it was ugly and had an odd jinking movement to it. When it flew into you, it would grab you, usually at your exposed neck, and clamp on with those sharp claws. You would, naturally, reach back and smack it but it had the consistency of soft butter and would smear all over you neck when you hit it. We found out later that it was something called a Mole Cricket and relatively harmless, but it sure seemed dangerous (and disgusting) at the time. There was also the bug we called the "One Pound Beetle" that was actually an Atlas Beetle and it was really large – even if it really didn't weigh a pound – but it was black and the head had three hard and sharp horns and it was about five inches long and about three and a half inches wide and when it flew, it made a loud buzzing sound and was a really unwelcome surprise when it flew into you. Their legs had these funny Flash Gordon fins on them, and their undersides were covered in a type of brownish fur, and they were in turn infested with mites, which made them repulsive to handle. I had one of these large beetles land at my Recorder's table one evening and when I saw those mites all over it, I doused it with lighter fluid – thinking that it would just kill the mites – but it also killed the beetle. I decided to keep the dead beetle as a paperweight but around midnight a drunk radio operator came into my tent and when he saw my beetle, he asked if he could have it. I gave it to him, and he stuck that huge insect into his trouser pocket and went off to his tent to sleep. About 0500 in the morning, I heard a bloodcurdling scream, and it was that radio operator when he woke up and found that beetle in his pocket.

We had a very small variety of ant too we called "Piss Ants" that were black and red but despite their small size, they were awesome in their meat-eating capabilities. If you killed a rat and left him where he lay, the Piss Ants would stream to the rat and by morning, a completely cleaned skeleton was all that was left.

We also had scorpions, giant venomous centipedes, huge spiders, leeches in the water and wet grass, and probably hundreds of other species and they all lived with us wherever we were in Vietnam. Yeesh.

I was assigned to a 155mm howitzer again and with a tall gunnery sergeant with a waxed handlebar mustache, towed that gun to a South Vietnamese Army artillery position at PK17, 17 km north of Hue. PK17 was a large cantonment surrounded completely by the deepest and tallest barbed wire barriers I had ever seen and in front of that, minefields. Neither the Gunny nor I spoke any Vietnamese (and I didn't know very much about artillery), yet it was our job to train the Vietnamese gun crews on that weapon. Once again, my High School French kicked in (more or less) and we got going. The Vietnamese soldiers were very friendly and curious about us since none of them had met Americans before. They had one of their soldiers who was about a head taller than all the others (Vietnamese men were for the most part several inches shorter than we were) and they called him "the American" which they all thought was pretty funny; since that particular trooper was both large and stupid.

While we were there, everyone wanted to take us to their homes and feed us or in the Gunny's case, drink with him. One day a Vietnamese E-3 named Tranh Dinh Y invited me to go outside the cantonment to have dinner with his family and the Gunny approved the request. I walked with Y to his home about a kilometer away and Y hinted that it would be proper etiquette for me to shave before dinner – which to me was amusing, since I barely needed to shave at that point in my life. But he produced an old French safety razor, and I used a hand mirror outside his house to shave. I heard a lot of giggling and saw that there were dozens of kids watching me shave through the gaps in the thatching of the house walls.

We had a dinner which was exotic to me and not very palatable – barely boiled pieces of duck, and some salad sort of a thing with lettuce of some kind around jellied duck blood with peanuts. I realized that this was undoubtedly a feast to them, so I ate everything in front of me and thanked them afterward, quietly and manfully suppressing the impulse to throw up. When it was time to go, it was dark and raining hard, so Y and I put on our ponchos over our helmets and weapons and walked back. As we got closer to PK17, we walked on a trail that headed for the entrance through the minefield and the barbed wire. I saw a squad of Vietnamese approaching head on, framed by the flood-lights at PK17 and they passed us parallel to our trail without giving any notice of us. They were wearing ponchos like we were but were wearing round soft hats and didn't seem to be very uniform in their equipment or uniforms. As the last guy in their squad went by, I saw that he was carrying a Russian DP machine gun and I asked Y—"*Qui est là?*" and Y said, "*Taisez-vous: Ils ont VC!*" It seems that they had some sort of local truce going. I turned and was ready to fire my M-14 at them but they disappeared into the heavy rain. Probably wouldn't have been a good idea, anyway.

Schoolgirls on bicycles, wearing the traditional Ao Dai dress (Photo by Ramon R. Alba used with permission)

Loading up ammunition at the Perfume River in Hue City. (Photo by Ramon R. Alba, used with permission)

When we got back to Phu Bai, my main job was driving artillery ammunition from Hue City, along the Perfume River where we loaded boxes and pallets of ammunition from navy landing craft and then brought them back to Phu Bai. My truck was loaded with as much 105mm ammunition as they could get on it, often higher than the rails on the truck, enough to make the truck squat down heavily at the rear and made it a challenge to steer straight on the road. The weather was clear but hot, so I used to open the pivoting sections of the windshield in front of me to let the fresh air pour in and I'd kick the foot pedals in the lower front of the cabin to open air panels to let more air in. On Highway 1, we were pretty safe from snipers and mines, but it did cross our minds that we'd make a really big bang if anybody wanted it to happen. I did several of these convoys and learned to navigate Hue well. It was a very lovely city, with a large white Catholic cathedral, a university with lots of pretty girl students with long black hair, wearing white Ao Dais, pedaling their bicycles around it; a massive iron bridge across the Perfume River and an ancient fortress called "the Citadel." I really wanted to spend some time looking at Hue on foot, but that wasn't allowed. I just could drive alongside the huge moat around the Citadel and look at its massive walls from the outside. On the way into Hue one day in early April, I heard gunshots and when I turned a corner, I saw two women dressed in black, lying in the street. I stopped to see if I could help, and we put bandages on them and then loaded them into the back of my truck and drove to Alpha Med at Phu Bai. When we got there, one was dead but the other younger one was still alive. I never found out who shot them.

The battery would head out from Phu Bai to nearby areas farther West for one day fire missions and my job after we arrived in these field positions was to take an M60 machine gun and take up a section of the battery defensive perimeter. After the Gunny had indicated where I was supposed to setup and what my fields of fire were to be, we would dig the position in, emplace the machine gun, and then build a poncho roof over our position – and then eat. We were facing large fields with kids tending water buffalos and very quickly those same kids were invading our machine gun position, begging for candy and cigarettes (all the kids smoked) and very soon, we had about thirty kids there. While I was trying to convince them to leave us alone, one of the kids, a boy about 10 years old, had taken our machine gun completely apart and had all the pieces laid out neatly on one of our ponchos.

That really got my attention and I demanded that he put it back together – quick before anybody from the battery saw this – and he did it; put it all together, loaded a belt of ammunition and offered to fire it! I have no idea at all how that kid knew how to field-strip and operate an M60, but he definitely knew it well.

I didn't let him fire it and then one of the NCOs came out and saw the crowd of kids and started yelling "get them out of here!"

I told the kids to leave ("Di Dai"). They yelled "Di Dai" back at me. I threw a small rock in their direction, and they threw about thirty rocks back in my direction. The kids were having a great time – much more interesting than tending buffalo – and their aim got better; so I finally taught them that I could throw farther than they could, and they finally left, still in fine humor. Of course, after that I discovered that they had gotten all of our C-rations and we didn't get our lunch. Cute kids. My main worries were that I'd really get in trouble if they stayed with us and that they'd be in the middle of things if the enemy hit us.

On the way back to my truck as I carried the M60 over my shoulder, I heard a "whuff" and when I looked up, I saw a huge water buffalo with its head down, pawing the ground directly in front of me. I was a city kid, but the intentions of that monster were obvious, even to me. I put the M60 into my shoulder, made sure that ammo belt was clear and pushed the safety off to try to stop that thing when it charged.

Then I felt a pair of whacks to my left calf and looked down to see a little girl – maybe 5 or 6 years old – with a short bamboo switch in her hand saying, "no, no, no." I was startled into relaxing my trigger finger as she ran up to that bull buffalo and whacked its rear leg with the switch. The buffalo immediately calmed down, turned away from me, and started to eat again.

Humbled, I re-shouldered my machine gun and walked the rest of the way back to my truck.

Back at Phu Bai at about March 10th, we watched as helicopters brought in scores of men, many of them wounded, from a battle at the Special Forces camp at A Shau. They were dirty and wore distinctive "Tiger Stripe" utility uniforms with a small, round-brimmed hat and I saw several of those big guys crying. From what I could hear, it was an enormous battle against North Vietnamese Regulars and the survivors were lucky to get out.

Very soon after, there was some sort of crisis for the Vietnamese government involving the Buddhists. When I was sent out for another ammunition convoy, this time in charge of a serial of five trucks, we ran into obstacles in the middle of Highway 1—meant to block our traffic north. The obstacles were what we called "family altars." The Vietnamese homes all had a wooden stand in their homes with photos of their deceased relatives and they would burn incense in front of the pictures.

Those altars were in the street, one in front of each of the homes bordering Highway 1 near Hue. I decided to thread my way carefully between those altars, snaking that 5 Ton and trailer carefully around each one and the other four trucks of my serial behind me exactly followed me. After a short distance doing this, families in front of us moved their altars out of the way and waved cheerfully at us.

When we got into Hue, we were soon blocked by a huge crowd of people filling a large square with thousands of people. Very soon, all of my trucks were enveloped into the crowd, and we were stuck there among them. Since there really wasn't anything we could do – we had no communication with anyone and were only barely armed – we just climbed up on our hoods and watched the demonstration. There were banners and songs and lots of yelling we didn't understand so we kept quiet and nonthreatening to just wait things out. It was a huge sea of people, filling a large square and all the roads leading from the square. While we sat there, an older woman in a conical straw hat came up to my truck and started to yell something at me while the crowd around me watched. I waited until she took a breath and then I imitated her tone and volume and yelled gibberish back at her, complete with the same fist gesture she had used. The crowd laughed and that made Cone Hat Lady madder. She spat up at me and smiling, I pretended to spit back at her. Then she picked up a small rock and threw it at me. I caught the rock in my hand and carefully aimed it at the edge of her hat and knocked it off her head. The crowd laughed harder and then opened a path for our five trucks to continue on, away from the demonstration.

Two things happened in mid-April: my truck driver's license was torn up and we went to the site of a battle. The way I lost my license was that I had come to the attention of the battery Executive Officer (XO), Lieutenant Z, several times and he was losing patience with me (it didn't help that I often beat him in chess). I had accidently holed the engine pan once, running over an invisible obstacle, and I had driven my truck into an unoccupied mortar pit because I couldn't see it from my angle in the driver's seat and didn't have anyone guiding me on the ground. The last straw was when I backed into the only communications pole in Phu Bai and knocked out phone communications for a wide area.

Lt. Z held a formal battery formation, called me out from the ranks and with great ceremony, tore my government driver's license into small bits. Everyone thought it was very funny, but I was shocked and for a short while, homeless. I wasn't a member of the motor pool, or any other section and I didn't have any job at all.

Just that night, we were told to get the battery ready to CSMO (Close Station, March Order – or in our vernacular, "Collect S__t, Move Out"). Unusually, we were told to tie coils of barbed wire to the outside rails of the trucks, and we were issued ammunition and grenades and we moved at night south towards Danang to a gun position that had been previously occupied by another Marine 105mm battery. We rolled in, and the place was a mess, and some wreckage was still there. The word was that that battery had been overrun and there were all sorts of rumors of heavy casualties and of howitzers and bunkers destroyed before the enemy was driven off.

We were sobered by the evidence of casualties and damage and even more that the enemy had successfully pulled it off – up to that point, we had considered ourselves invulnerable.

We emplaced our guns in the same firing positions, repaired the barbed wire and bunkers and resumed fire support for the area. I still didn't have a home, but when I saw a squad being prepared for local patrolling, I picked up an M60 machine gun and ammunition and went out with them (nobody else wanted to carry the heavier machine gun). We went out a couple of kilometers from the battery position almost straight west and approached a medium-size village of homes built up on stilts. As the lieutenant turned the squad in towards the village to look it over, I was posted on a piece of high ground overlooking them with my machine gun. In a few minutes, the lieutenant signaled me to come to where he was. When I got there, a prosperous-looking, middle-aged man was talking loudly to the lieutenant and the lieutenant asked me to try to find out what he was saying. Once again, High School French paid off and the gentleman started talking rapidly to me in French. He was asking us to come inside his large home and to eat dinner with them. The lieutenant and I went inside with another Marine and the guy never stopped chattering at us. There was a large family sitting at a long table with some food on it and they stared at us with obvious apprehension. The man kept vigorously gesturing at us to go ahead and sit at the table, but we stayed where we were, watching. The man came up to me and pulled me by my arm towards a side room and talking continuously, pointed at a young, smiling and naked young Vietnamese woman lying on a bed and indicated that I should go in there with her.

Now, I don't know how you would have reacted, but the hair stood up on the back of my neck and I said to the lieutenant: "It's a trap! Let's get out of here!" We hustled out the door and down the ladder and out of the village. It was very clearly a dangerous area for us.

In the battery, we improved our defenses, since it was obvious that it was still a really hostile area, and it was only a matter of time before the enemy went at us. Each morning we would inspect our barbed wire and every morning, we would find bare footprints <u>inside</u> our barbed wire barriers in the areas we had carefully raked before nightfall. After a couple of weeks sweating it, another battery came to our position, and we worked to transition it to their control. One of the items they brought was a new device called a Patrol Seismic Intrusion Device (PSID) that had a headset and a set of wires and sensors that branched out in several directions to sense movement. We didn't think that it really worked well when we tested it, but they were emplaced around the position anyway. The incoming battery commander also insisted on installing floodlights at the corners of the perimeter, which to my Lance Corporal mind was idiocy. Lights at night? Seemed like madness because it seemed as though the last thing you'd ever want, would be to illuminate yourself for the enemy to shoot.

Shows what I knew. A couple of weeks after we left, the new battery was attacked and the PSIDs warned them that the enemy was there and the searchlights handily illuminated the enemy recoilless rifle crews before they could fire, and they annihilated the enemy attacking force. It was all written up in the *Stars and Stripes* newspaper afterward.

From the start of my story until this point, the enemy activity seemed desultory, with the occasional ambush or sniping. The night attack against the battery we replaced was a turning point in the war for us in Bravo Battery as the enemy became more aggressive and their numbers were more obviously greater than we knew.

The pontoon bridge connecting the road from Danang to Hill 55 and Anderson trail. The blown bridge is slightly visible to the left and the Marine in the water is supposed to be guarding the bridge – not floating around on his "Rubber Lady" (air mattress). (Photo by Ramon R. Alba, used with permission)

Fort Bravo

By this time, I had been "adopted" by Gun Section 5 as an "On the Job Trainee Artilleryman"; so I had a home again. Our new position was somebody else's old position on a short hilltop, an island of white sand above vast rice paddies in all directions. Framing all of those rice paddies were heavy tree lines and within those dense tree lines were scattered village complexes, long established trail systems, a Catholic church, some old graveyards with concrete tombstones and at the far edge, a river hidden behind the trees to the west. The village complexes near us were An Trach, Cam Ne, and Xuan Diem and their names would become etched in our memories. There was a river between our position and Hill 55 and ominously, the VC had blown the bridge into the water, and we had a pontoon bridge that we had to use to reach Hill 55 or the Anderson Trail, the route to the 1st Marines headquarters. We named that position "Fort Bravo," eventually even building a sign with that name at the entrance into the battery position.

My duties were simple at first: Ammunition Man. 105mm ammunition came in a wooden crate with rope handles at both ends. It contained two full rounds each and weighed 120 pounds and most of the ammunition we had was made during WWII. Believe it or not, even though we normally loaded those things on the truck using two men – one on each rope handle – we were strong young men, and we quickly perfected a technique where we would grab a box by ourselves, snatch it up to chest height and then, whipping your whole body, throw it into the back of the truck. Once you had developed the muscles and technique to do that trick, you could actually throw that box hard enough to reach the end of the truck bed, against the cab of the truck. When you broke the flat steel bands that sealed the cases (usually with an axe), the two rounds were enclosed within creosote-soaked four inch diameter black fiber tubes with metal caps. You opened the tubes either by pulling two yellow fabric tapes on the sides of the tubes – or you used the axe again to knock the metal caps at the end off. Depended on how much time you had to open the ammunition tube. If things were slow, you had plenty of time to unwrap things carefully and stow them in ready bunkers by the guns. But if you were firing frantically to support some unit in trouble out there and you needed ammunition immediately, you used the axes frantically to keep up. There were some days where we exceeded 500 rounds per gun per day and rarely even 1,000 rounds per gun when units were in trouble and needed the weight and relentlessness of our artillery fire. On those days and sometimes even nights, we ran continuous convoys up the road to Danang to get more ammunition. Everyone, even the office clerks, cooks, the officers and even the Chaplain would be breaking out and preparing ammunition on those days.

My first Section Chief was Sgt H (Nickname "Habu" – a type of aggressive and poisonous Okinawan snake), a skinny, bent, older NCO with a sour personality. He spent a lot of his time complaining quietly under his breath at us and he was distinctly afraid of our rifles around him. He would start violently if you chambered a round near him while you were preparing to move in convoy or to go out on patrol. He did not train us. Or talk to us. If he was proficient at his craft, Habu kept it to himself. His version of leadership was to snarl and point at what he wanted to be done. It was up to us to figure out what he wanted us to do and get it done.

While I am on the subject of the older NCOs, most of those that we had in Bravo Battery were real lemons. They only seemed to be around to enforce petty rules and to give out punishment to those they didn't like. A lot of the time, many of them just stayed in their tents and drank. A couple of them were Korean War vets and they obviously knew their way around a war, but we rarely got any instruction from them – we were either ignored with disdain or just given work to do, like filling sandbags or emplacing barbed wire, sent out on outpost or guard, or moving ammunition and supplies. They never participated in any work and most of the time, they didn't even watch us do it. They gave us the job and we did it with very little affection either way. The low point with our Battery Gunnery Sergeant occurred when he used a shotgun to chase down, maim and then kill a kitten that we had kept in our gun position. We despised him even more after that.

Our officers were OK; the battery commander was Captain C and he was a hands-on guy and visible a lot of the time. I met him the day he took over while I was working on an ammunition party. He came over to me and said, "I hear that you're a s__tbird, Lindsey" I looked at him angrily and said, "I am sure as hell not a s__tbird, Sir!" (a worthless goof off), and he smiled and said that he'd keep an eye on me anyway. I took that as a sort of apology and smiled back – I may have only been a lowly Lance Corporal "OJT Cannoneer" and a failed truck driver, but I was proud of my work anyway. And I didn't have the Clap.

Lieutenant Z was tall and looked like a former football player and as Executive Officer (XO) of the battery had the greatest day-to-day power and contact with us lowly enlisted swine. He was quite full of himself and occasionally would deign to play chess with me, since I was known to be pretty good. When he lost a game (which was almost every time) he would pick me up bodily and throw me out of the XO Pit (the battery control center) with my chess set flying out after me. Our battery officers were a bit like pompous older brothers.

Battery in convoy going through a small town
(Photo by Ramon R. Alba, with permission)

In early April, our battery was sent far south to the old fortress of Fai Fo, in An Hoa province. The area was beautiful, and the archeological ruins were amazing. There were also the remains of French positions in evidence. I had time to look around because my duties as a new cannoneer weren't very taxing and I tended to be a "combat tourist" instead of a committed warfighter at that stage.

At some point soon after, our battery occupied a position south of Phu Bai called "Position 10." When we got there, we were very surprised to see that there were revetments and trail pits (the slots in the ground cut to fit the spades at the back part of a howitzer that make it dig into the ground during recoil and keep it anchored there instead of running down the road). We were grateful, because Position 10 was on a hilltop on very hard, rocky ground – it was almost impossible to dig there and here, somebody, already did it for us – and had the same model 105mm howitzers that we did. Another oddity of Position 10 was that there was a small grove of thin trees at the top of the hill and around us but not growing anywhere else nearby. The rest of the hill was completely bare of any plant life.

We set up and fired there for a few days and in my capacity of being up for grabs, I was picked to build barbed wire barriers for the sides of our position. We formed a working party of eight Marines and once we were shown where to put the wire in, we hammered steel engineer stakes into the rock-hard soil and stretched barbed wire between them. It was hot, hard work and we were absorbed in it when a small green observation plane flew low over us. We looked at it briefly and enjoyed the impromptu air show. It flew over us again, lower. It had our attention, but we couldn't figure out why he was doing the low fly-bys. On the third pass, he flew directly over us, a hand emerged from an open side canopy panel and a note wrapped around a rock landed quite close to us. It read: "Hey stupid. Look East."

We looked east and there was a large VC patrol strung out in a line walking, as oblivious of us as we had been to them. We were all completely out in the open, no cover, about 200 meters away and we just watched them walk in a long line into a far tree line and out of sight. Reading this you'd be right to wonder why we didn't immediately open fire and obliterate the enemy. For one thing, because we were a wiring party, we only had a couple of rifles with very limited ammunition with us but the main reason was that this was the first time most of us had ever seen live VC out in the broad daylight before and we weren't 100% sure they weren't some sort of local Popular Forces militia.

Eventually, I puzzled out why there were these little trees on the top our hill. Position 10 was called "Position 10" because it was an old French artillery position and that was the name marked on our French Maps (many of the maps we had were old French maps). The position had obviously been heavily attacked at some point – there were "pineapple" grenade fragments all over the place, fired French 7.5mm cartridges strewn about and tellingly, mortar tails. A mortar tail is the largest piece of a mortar bomb left over after it explodes. Mortar rounds are fired nearly vertically and arrive even more vertically. The mortar Point Detonating fuze goes straight down several inches into the ground while the lethal steel fragments spray to the sides to shred anyone above ground. The tails fall intact after the explosion, and these had markings showing their Chinese and Russian origins. Clearly, the French battery in Position 10 had been heavily attacked and likely overrun – but the mortar fuze holes and craters left over were the only place a tree seed could enter that rocky soil and germinate so each tree grew where a Viet Minh mortar round had struck. It was eerie to hear the wind whispering through that little grove.

When that operation was finished, we moved back to our "Fort Bravo" position south of Danang.

That area was in the middle of one of the most active areas in Vietnam. We were just north of Hill 55, where the infantry regiment was sited and we were in the middle of the main infiltration route from the Ho Chi Minh Trail, through the A Shau Valley and funneled right towards us in the path of Danang and its important airfield. I researched the number of dead the Marine Corps sustained in Vietnam – 14,844 – and about 10,000 of those lost were killed in that area, between us and An Hoa. We called it "Dodge City" and it wasn't until long after the war was over that I found out that whole platoons of Marines had been annihilated in the area around us, often by specialized "Main Force" Vietcong units like R20 Battalion.

We fired our 105s almost without break there, day and night. Most of the time, it was fire missions in support of some grunt unit who had found the enemy – or they had found us – and since that happened all day, we fired all day. At night we'd fire H&I (Harassment and Interdiction) fires at spots, like trail intersections or possible staging areas that were designated by our superiors. For those, we'd use the H&I list with its firing data and times, set the gun on the firing data and set the charge for the rounds; then at the appointed time, load and fire. This, unfortunately, was done by young Lance Corporals late at night and unsupervised, so inevitably boredom would cause some of the gunners to stick razor blades between the fuze and the projectile body to make the projectile scream when it was fired or insert a rat in the powder canister to send him downrange as incandescent gas. As much fun as it was for the experimenters, the price for fiddling with the projectiles was a change in achieved range and that 33-pound piece of explosive and steel landed somewhere other than where it was intended. But we never thought that far.

Now a word about the enemy forces we dealt with. They came in three varieties:

The "Local VC"– Vietcong fighters from the local area who were marginally trained, armed with older weapons, often bolt-action rifles and they primarily added mass to the Main Force units, scouted, provided logistic support, and emplaced mines and booby traps. They were in the main, poor shots and escaped as soon as you engaged them. They surrendered readily when they were trapped. Most of them had a day job, usually farmer or fisherman and unless they were armed in their day job, we left them alone. Oddly, most VC were readily recognizable by their haircuts. It was a distinctive "long on top, with a rapid taper from the bottom" look that aided us in identifying them.

The Main Force or "Hard Core" VC– these were the tough professionals, they were politically rabid, and merciless. Some of them had fought the French as Viet Minh and were extensively experienced and vicious. There were cases where we found some of our men tortured and murdered after they had been captured by them. They were the ones going into the villages at night to kill anyone who stood up to them – it was common to see a village elder's head on a pole with a message written by the VC assassination team on a piece of cardboard – to kidnap and recruit, stage political propaganda sessions, plan and prepare for night attacks and raids, mortar, rocket, and recoilless rifle attacks. They were meticulous in their planning, often using sand models of our positions for their assault teams. They almost never took prisoners, killing our wounded when they overran us and when they did take prisoners it was only to torture and then kill them later. They were often armed with our weapons.

The last group was the North Vietnamese Army or NVA (or "Hard Hats" because of their distinctive pith helmets). They had good uniforms and equipment including the latest Soviet small arms; they had conventional organizations and were well-fed, courageous, and in good physical condition. They had excellent training and good fire discipline. They rarely surrendered and they generally respected our medics and we generally respected theirs. Their packs were so much better than ours that they became a prized item to capture. Some NVA units even had heavy mortars, howitzers, antiaircraft guns, and even tanks. They always came in battalion strength at minimum (about 600 men). If you thought that you had found a platoon of NVA, you were wrong, because they always came in battalions or greater strength. A lot of units learned that lesson the hard way.

For some reason, our press insisted that the NVA wasn't in South Vietnam and later in the war when it became even more obvious, they refused to believe that the NVA had tanks and artillery. I guess they should have asked us.

Now a bit about us, the Marines in those early days. We still had the older green cotton sateen utility uniform, black leather boots – (which quickly abraded to a shabby greyish-tan), M1955 Flak Jacket (body armor – which had heavy fiberglass plates inside—which had a label on the inside that offered the excuse that this "vest will stop 70% of bullets and fragments"; so if you were killed by the remaining 30%, it wasn't their fault); a WWII steel helmet with reversible camouflage cloth cover; a WWII-era cartridge belt, medical kit, canteens, packs, shelter halves and as I mentioned earlier, our rations were ancient canned stuff by the "Blue Star Food Manufacturing Inc." from 1942 (each with a small pack of 5 cigarettes inside). I always promised myself that I'd find out who Blue Star Food Manufacturing Inc. was and force them at gunpoint to eat their greasy, bad smelling "mystery meat" products. In 1966, we still had the M-14 rifle which is a great old-fashioned steel and wood beast that was long and heavy and difficult to control in full-auto but it always fired when you pulled the trigger and hit what you were aiming at—all the way out to 500 meters and beyond. It would rust in Vietnam's humid and hot climate, but rust didn't interfere with its reliability or its deadly power. The constant scrubbing of scale rust made them almost bare of any finish in a little while. We used to joke about our "chrome rifles." Some of you who are very observant will note that Marine helmets of that time have a worn section at the top of them and almost everyone has the camouflage cloth almost shredded there. The reason? We sat in our helmets. Since there were rarely things to sit on in the field, we would turn our helmets over and sit in them rather than sit flat on the ground. That wore the tops of the helmet covers in a distinctive pattern. We also used our helmets as shaving bowls after we pulled the fiberglass liners out of them.

Most of the enlisted Marines came from Middle Class to Poor families from all over the country. Most were at least high school graduates and as I mentioned earlier, some came from the judicial system to avoid prison. We had the customs and prejudices and language of the '60s which was both good and bad. We were strong believers in our country, took the risks that were expected of us, and longed for home. We also had some of the foulest language, grossest habits and we smoked like chimneys: we got cigarettes for little or nothing and smoking cigars when you could find them was also popular. We had a unique way of smoking a cigarette by holding the lit end inward towards the palm, while cupping it with the other hand. That way its lit end did not illuminate your face at night and cause a bullet to be sent in your direction. We had one instance where a new guy lit a cigarette openly at night in our gun position and we slapped the lighter from his hand. He got angry and told us that he was "tired of hearing bulls__t from you old salts"; picked up his lighter and tried again. A rifle shot narrowly missed him by maybe a couple of feet or so and hit the recuperator cylinder at the top of the howitzer next to him, leaving a narrow scar in the steel.

The Gun 5 tent, with all the comforts of home: that's a mess tray in the center of the picture, a reel-to-reel tape player, desks and shelves made of ammunition boxes, and pictures out of Playboy and other magazines completing the décor. (Photo by Ramon R. Alba, used with permission)

This probably sounds like an exaggeration, but there were enemy snipers waiting outside our position all the time. We would lose people fairly regularly to some of the better snipers they had. You learned to make your out-of-cover movements fast and to another piece of cover even if you hadn't heard a sniper for a while. We even had one evening where every outpost was near-missed by someone firing a silenced rifle using some sort of night vision sight. We were in total darkness; yet we each heard the crack of a flying bullet go by, three feet or so to our left with no muzzle flash or sound of a shot. Fortunately for us, the sniper hadn't properly zeroed his weapon and didn't hit anyone that night.

Initially, our training and tactics were poorly matched to Vietnam's terrain and the enemy forces, and we had to adapt. We discovered that the local VC battalion was deliberately provoking us to deploy in lines when we made contact per our training and then firing down our flanks from hidden firing positions. We also faced a horrific and sadistic array of booby traps, mines, and stake-lined pits on every conceivable avenue of approach. The older vets taught us how to be aware and to be brave. We taught ourselves the unique and changing tactics of the day-to day slog against a well-hidden and relentless enemy. Those of us who adapted and learned generally survived and kept of our bodies intact. Slow learners didn't.

We stayed at Fort Bravo, our well-developed position near Hill 55 through July and then our battery was packed up for the long convoy north to a huge, massed artillery position near Dong Ha. There were battalion after battalion of 105s, 155s and even 8 Inch guns (203mm) and long-range army 175mm guns, all sited near each other and oriented North, for firing in support of Operation Hastings, the first engagement against NVA divisions near the Demilitarized Zone (DMZ).

The Northern part of South Vietnam below the DMZ was very mountainous and heavily wooded. The Ben Hai River was the geographic boundary between North Vietnam and South Vietnam and a 5 kilometer buffer on either side of the river was the DMZ, a "no man's land." The North Vietnamese Army had infiltrated across the DMZ and the First Marine Division was going to oppose them.

**The Author, perched on Gun 5 near Cam Lo during Operation Hastings.
(Photo from the Author's Collection)**

For my part of things, I was almost always involved in ammunition parties to keep our battery supplied while we fired almost continuous fire missions at the enemy while our infantry was in contact. I didn't drive the truck this time – I just went to the ammunition dumps, loaded as many boxes as could be fit on the truck; then rode back to the battery sitting on top of those boxes, and then unloaded them. The guns fired them as fast as they arrived, so we worked to exhaustion, day after day.

Crossing the Perfume River through Hue City, full load of howitzer ammunition and a guard in back (Photo by Ramon R. Alba, used with permission)

One of those trips, when I got back into the battery position, I saw three of our battery's six guns firing northward with three muzzle flashes visible in a cloud of dust and three more muzzle flashes aimed to the south. I went to the XO and asked him what kind of fire mission that was, and he stuck his head out of the tent and yelled: "Check firing! Check firing"! It turned out that three of the six guns' Section Chiefs had misread their M12 sights and were firing the exact reverse of their firing data. While we were worrying about where those rounds actually went, a 155mm Illumination round went off almost directly above us. An Illumination Round is a hollow projectile with a magnesium parachute flare in it. When the time fuze goes off, the back of the projectile is ejected, and the flare and parachute come out and the flare ignites. Usually, those are fired at night to light up some part of the battlefield but this one was fired to get our attention: it turned out that our mis-aimed rounds came near to a South Vietnamese artillery battery, so they sent something non-lethal towards us to get our attention. The funny part of this story is that illumination rounds have a small, curved aluminum protector plate inside to keep the parachute from being burned by the ejection charge. That plate falls clear when the parachute comes out and, in this case, fell a few thousand feet to hit directly between the First Sergeant and the Battery Gunnery Sergeant's butts as they sat on the "four holer" boxes that served as our communal bathroom. The box broke and both of them landed in the deep pool of excrement below. We were not displeased – remember the kitten? I've always said that: "God has a sense of humor and a precise aim."

On one of the ammo runs, we had to cross a small river over a bridge that had been destroyed at least three times before. Our truck slowly crossed over concrete parts, the steel sections, the wood planks in the middle. While we were gingerly crossing the wood part, I spotted a sinuous movement in the brown water below and shot it several times – and the Marines who were supposed to be guarding the bridge but were swimming farther downstream started yelling. Then they spotted what I had shot: a smallish crocodile (about 5 feet, nose to tail tip). We hauled it out of the water and threw it up in our ammo stack on the truck and took it to the battery position to show everyone.

When I tossed it to the ground, Lt Z came up and said—"Wow – an alligator!"

I said: "No Sir, it's a crocodile – you know, long thin snout, teeth start all the way back and … it's Asia."

Lt Z came straight up to me, towered over me and said, "Lance Corporal, if I tell you it's an alligator, it's an alligator!"

I took out my canteen, walked over to the dead crocodile and poured water over it in a cross. I said, "I baptize thee alligator" and then turned to Lt. Z and said, "you're right Sir – it's an alligator!"

You can probably tell why I wasn't in line for Corporal anytime soon.

About this time, July 1966, the rains really arrived. It rained a lot before, but nothing like this! It arrived behind a dust storm, a dark wall approaching behind it and then for a few seconds, it was falling mud and then endless rain. It rained steadily and relentlessly for months. Not just showers, but pounding, powerful rushing rain that soaked everything and everyone to the skin. It was the arrival of the Monsoon season, that time of the year where everything comes to a stop as the rice paddies flood and overflow; the rivers expand and fill, and all the creepy-crawly creatures come to share our hilltops with us – except the war goes steadily on. There was no relief, no place to escape from the wet. Your carefully protected photographs or books or other keepsakes rotted and melted away, your fine items like cameras developed mold and became useless and patrolling became an exercise to not drowning. You learned to just accept the misery and continue on—wet when you wake, wet all day, wet when you go to sleep, wet on the outside as you were on the inside. We would take our clothes off, walk out of our tents, soap up, then just stand there as the powerful rain rinsed the soap off.

One day during either Operation Hastings or Prairie (Like I said earlier, we never knew when one operation started and ended. Nobody told us a damn thing.), I was shown an NVA lieutenant who had surrendered. Since nobody knew what he was saying and there were no Vietnamese in our position, they thought I could talk to him. He spoke reasonable French, so it turned out that we could talk. He was kind of small and wimpy looking and had those French shaded glasses where they were dark transparent blue at the top and became clearer towards the center and then completely clear at the bottom of the lenses. I took him to a truck in our position and draped a poncho over the windshield to hide the candle I lit above the dashboard, and we talked in a combination of schoolboy French, hand signs and drawn pictures on a pad most of the night. I asked him why he surrendered, and he said that he had been a railroad engineer and been drafted into the North Vietnamese Army. He had gone through training in Xuan My and then sent south on the Ho Chi Minh Trail. He had been told that "the south would welcome them as liberators" but he said the southern villages had hidden their food (and their daughters) and were hostile to them. He said that his units had been repeatedly bombed and that the southerners clearly preferred the Americans to them. He got discouraged about all that and surrendered, bringing an AK-47 rifle with him. Later that night, we talked about motorcycles, and it turned out that he had the same kind of Honda 305 that I did.

The huge battles that developed during Operation Hastings and the follow-on Operation Prairie lasted through September while the Monsoons continued, and we were awash in mud all of the time. We had heard of some of the incredible fighting that had been going on and we were sobered but committed to doing as much as we could to support our infantry. Day after day, we saw the medical evacuation flights going over us and we knew that we had lost a lot of men. I started to feel that I wasn't taking on my share of the war, having it relatively safe in the artillery while the infantry was facing daily Hell.

At some point we went to a Montagnard village and we were able to visit a home. They were shy, very dark- skinned people that lived in homes built on stilts and were obviously very poor. All of their women were deeply tanned and topless which was a bit startling, but their simplicity and dignity made us careful not to stare.

When the operations Hastings and Prairie were over, we joined huge, miles-long convoys south to return to our position near Hill 55. At some point north of Hue, the convoy stopped, and we heard gunfire toward the front of the convoy and saw two Air Force B-57s flying in tall round loops, each at opposite points of the loop, firing at some point ahead of us. Then I heard a huge bang, and my eye captured the flash image of two F-8 Crusaders flying just over us, so fast that it sounded like a thunderclap. They were firing their cannon at the ambush in front of us and they actually seemed to bank to avoid hitting us in our trucks, they were so low as they flashed over us.

We passed the burned wreckage of some ARVN vehicles and large burned areas in the brush along the road when we continued south again.

On the way north to the DMZ before and now as we headed south, we passed several French concrete cupolas and bunkers that they had constructed during their colonial war. It was eerie passing them and it made you wonder how effective hiding in those things would have been and impressed you with the permanence of concrete. Those things will be there a thousand years, populated by the poor ghosts that built them and manned them.

We returned to Fort Bravo near Hill 55 and resumed our fire support there.

Around this time, we got 1st Lieutenant O as our new Battery XO. He was a tall, serious, and energetic man and a strong leader. The XO of a firing battery in those days had a small Command Post (CP) tent in the center front of the battery, just behind the gunline, and he was the man who ran the firing of the guns. In those early, nondigital days, he would hold his hand high in the air when the guns were laid and ready to fire and yell; "Battery! Staaand Byyy – FIRE!" and the guns all fired as one. If they didn't, he'd yell—"get it together Girls!" He was the hardest-working officer in the battery, and we tried to keep out of his way.

Oddly, it seems as though a Vietcong unit had used our position while we were up north because we found 25,000 rounds of Chinese pistol ammunition in one of our ammo bunkers! That came in handy later when we had a captured NVA K-50 submachinegun to shoot.

Gun 5 with its well-developed firing position just north of Hill 55 at "Fort Bravo". (Photo by Ramon R. Alba, used with permission)

The XO Pit, with a BC Scope on an ammo box platform. The red and white painted pole in the center is one of the two aiming stakes for one of the howitzers. (Photo by Ramon R. Alba, used with permission)

In Section 5, I had advanced from Ammunition Man to Assistant Gunner to Gunner and I did well in my ad hoc cannoneer career. The gun Section Chief was now Sergeant A now that the despised "Habu" was gone, and we had such characters as Corporal A in our section. We got along well together, and we had our own sandbagged wood-framed GP tent to call home. We decorated the interior of our tent with the big foldout photos of nearly naked (and heavily airbrushed) women from *Playboy* and other such sources and we held card games and chess tourneys when we weren't working on the gun, firing, standing outpost or out on working parties. We had a long, narrow trench next to our tent to dive into during mortar attacks and we really considered that we had all the comforts of home. Well, most of them. Cpl. A quickly became (and still is) my best friend. He was very well read and had read all of the books about Vietnam I had, and he was crazily creative. He designed and painted the Bravo Battery emblem – two crossed antique cannons with a green dragon intertwining them with a white shield at the center with a black Gothic B in the center of that. He was always inventing stuff. He once requested to use an M-14 rifle that had been run over by a bulldozer and bent right in front of the gas system. With the help of a welder, he built it into an effective and very fast-firing gravity fed machine gun for our perimeter. Marines from all around came to see Cpl. A's ersatz machine gun blazing away. He is the one who got me started going on the daily security patrols.

Gun 5 tent with Cpl. A's Battery Emblem in front. The sandbagged circle in the foreground is an 81mm mortar pit. (Photo by Ramon R. Alba, used with permission)

As I said earlier, our battery was perched on a flat-topped sand hill surrounded by acres of rice paddies. In a nearly circular fringe around those rice paddies were dense tree lines filled partially by villages. The patrols we carried out were conducted in the morning and afternoon and led by a Staff Sergeant. The 13 of us would leave the perimeter, cross the paddies, and skirt the edges of the tree lines, looking for signs of enemy activity, such as fighting positions or trenches or aiming stakes. Sometimes we'd enter the tree lines, going out of sight of our battery and into profoundly greater danger. The enemy was there, and we were always seen. The paths were often mined; their firing positions hidden within the underbrush and bunkers behind them.

The feeling that I had, just as we were leaving the safety of our barbed wire perimeter was a combination of fear and excitement. The second we crossed the wire, we would chamber rounds in our rifles, making that distinctive slick sound a round makes entering the chamber, and you'd know that you were on your own at that point and your heart rate would accelerate. Even though we were mere artillerymen imitating infantry, we kept a wide interval between us and approached the tree lines on the opposite side of the open rice paddies around us warily and completely focused.

We could always tell when things were going to get ugly because the villagers and livestock were nowhere to be seen and even the birds and the insects stopped singing. The enemy in our area seem to have used us a "training aids" and would conduct textbook ambushes on us fairly often. The firefight would start with sudden bursts of fire or a mine detonation and we would shoot back with everything we had and beat a fast retreat back to the open paddies so our fellow artillerymen up the hill could join in and fire the 105mm howitzers to force the enemy back. On my first patrol, I found a suitcase full of enemy uniforms and blank Vietcong ("Vietnam Workers' Party") ID cards and a book of silhouettes of American armored vehicles. Later I realized how lucky I was to have picked up something like that suitcase and not been blown to bits! Damn things like that were almost always booby-trapped to catch unwary idiots like me. Pretty convincing proof of enemy activity, though. During another patrol, we found a bunker that some VC had run into. We called for them to surrender in English and French but no response, so I put a blasting cap and fuse into a two pound block of C-4 explosive, primed it and threw it into the embrasure of the bunker—yelling "fire in the hole!" I lay flat waiting for the blast and the

Staff Sergeant grabbed the top of my flak jacket and the seat of my pants and dragged me farther away. When the charge went off, the whole top of that log bunker blew straight up in the air and the logs landed about where I had been.

"Checking IDs" during a local security sweep. Note the excellent dispersion between the troops; not bad for artillerymen! Also note the sling on that M-14: it uses a blanket roll strap to lengthen it and position the rifle at a convenient angle for fast use. Note the gravestones at the upper left of this photo. (Photo by Ramon R. Alba, used with permission)

We started to take casualties during these patrols. We'd take one or two wounded every other day and the enemy units were being more aggressive against us. One patrol, led by Sgt. H (who was promoted to sergeant earlier that day) turned his squad into the tree line and spotted what he thought was a VC half concealed in a fighting hole. He put his Marines on line and approached the "VC" which was really a dummy, covering a large parabolic shaped Claymore mine (Claymore mines were slabs of explosive faced with rows of steel ball bearings that were thrown at high velocity when the explosive was detonated). A hidden VC detonated the mine remotely, wounding almost everyone on that patrol, including Sgt. H. Back in the battery we heard the huge explosion, and we heard the call for help on the radio, calmly and clearly delivered by a blinded radio operator and their corpsman was tending the wounded when our relief force got to them, even though "doc" had lost his left arm.

Despite this almost daily bit of combat around us, we carried on our continuous firing in support of the Marine infantry around us. We were fast, accurate, and ready night or day – which added to our value as a target. We started getting mortar rounds in position soon after and we had a persistent sniper or two that harried us. We built more defenses and dug deeper holes and kept going.

Oddly, we also conducted civic action projects during some of these patrols outside our perimeter. It started in a large village to the southwest of us where we saw some kids with eye infections and some women who had cuts or small injuries. Our corpsman decided to hold up the patrol for a little while to treat the ladies and the kids while we were there. The next time we were in that village again, there were dozens of sick and lightly injured people there waiting for us; so we treated as many as we could, and we told them that we'd be there every Thursday from then on. On every Thursday morning patrol, we'd bring two corpsmen and as much medicine and bandages as we could carry and we'd get right to treating people, often most of the day. The enemy didn't attack us on these patrols and even started sending young men with the distinctive VC haircut to us get treated for small missile wounds and infections.

We told Captain C what was happening and asked him if we should be treating the enemy wounded and he said that we should keep doing it, "since the sniper fire has dropped way off since you started your program." I have a photo taken during one of these medical stops that shows our corpsman standing next to an older and very serious man in a VC field uniform. Everybody – villagers in particular – were afraid of this guy, and we suspect that he was the local VC Main Force commander, but he wasn't armed, and we had a sort of truce going; so nothing happened except for the photo. It has to be unique in the history of warfare to have a photograph like that. I've had people ask me why we didn't kill him or capture him, but we were in the middle of a sort of truce, more or less, out of sight of our battery or anyone else and there were only thirteen of us in the middle of enemy territory; didn't seem to be the smart thing to do.

"Doc" and the VC. (Photo by Ramon R. Alba, used with permission)

We also started to get the first hints that things weren't going well at home. Newspapers sent to us and what few magazines we had started to feature antiwar demonstrations and the tone of the articles began to question what we were doing there. While we were on patrol, we would find well-printed leaflets placed in a foot-long piece of split bamboo that told us that the war wasn't supported in the US and they would name some famous personality who was against the war. Many of those leaflets were printed in the US and sent to the enemy to be left for us.

The XO decided to do something about the huge number of rats that were living within our perimeter and announced to everyone that whoever gets the most confirmed rat kills in a given week would be allowed to drink all the Carling Black Label beer they could for one evening. The Carling beer was on a pallet in the corner of our position and since this was the pre-aluminum can days, the cans were steel and rusting – and uncooled, so the beer would be consumed British-style at an unappealing 80-90 degrees ambient temperature. The competition was ferocious and sometimes very dangerous: I saw a Warrant Officer from the Survey Section chasing rats through the position with a Thompson submachinegun, firing wildly and I saw another officer swing a machete at more rats. Cpl. A took a scientific approach and mounted electric blasting caps on boards with a battery and some C-Ration cheese as bait. His "rat mines" worked well but kept all of us on edge with the sudden explosions all over the place and half rats distributed widely. I won, though. I sent a letter to my parents earlier asking for Victor rat traps and they sent me two and they were very effective. Vietnamese rats apparently had never evolved a suspicion of things mechanical with cheese and they literally stood in line waiting for their chance to be killed by those things. I had very large rat try to drag off the body of a freshly killed medium-size rat and it backed into my reset trap, losing his life. Winning was fine, but I didn't like Carling Black Label beer in rusting cans, so somebody else got to drink that hot beer.

During one longer than usual patrol, while it was raining lightly, an army Huey helicopter circled our squad a couple of times, then landed in front of us. We were dumbfounded to see a middle-aged woman wearing army jungle fatigues covered with unit patches and badges and wearing a green beret.

She came closer to us and started to sing. She sang songs from the 1940s and she was very good, even though it was music more suited for our parents than us. She sang three songs, I think, the rain soaking all of us and when she finished, we tried to augment our applause by slapping our M-14 magazines together. Martha Rae got back into her helicopter and flew off and we were stunned and grateful for our own personal USO show. That was the only USO show I ever got to see while I was in Vietnam. I always wished that I could have thanked her again.

The XO asked me to write a response letter to a young woman named Sharon from the University of Michigan who had sent us a case of dog food with a note saying that it was for us "animals." He chose me to write back to her because I was less likely to send something nasty back. I thanked her for the dog food, telling her that it was great to have it for the pet dogs we had here (we didn't have any pets at all), ignoring the insult and I told her that we were proud to be helping the Vietnamese people. I got several letters more from Sharon, nice ones; so I must've been quite diplomatic. In one of her letters, she spoke about a new science fiction TV series called *Star Trek*. I eventually talked her into sending a picture of herself and she was really not my type, so our correspondence tapered off.

Our favorite patrol leader was Staff Sergeant D. He'd been in the Corps 16 years and was believed to be a Korean War combat veteran. He was competent and courageous and specialized in firing rifle grenades very accurately. The old-type M76 grenade launcher that attached to the muzzle of the M-14 used a blank cartridge to throw a full-size M26 frag grenade more than 100 meters and it took a lot of experience to fire that thing well. As with the other older Staff NCOs, D despised us younger Marines and barely spoke to us. But when he was leading a squad patrol, he was all business and directed us with skill. On one mid-day patrol in the Fall, we were just at the edge of our west flank tree line when he signaled for us to face west and move into the trees. I had the right flank of our squad, and I was facing a trail in front of me which meant easy going. But I noticed three things: there were thorn vines laced between the lines of trees on both sides of the trail, like a barbed wire fence and there were two felled trees at the far end of the trail in the form of an "X" – which I had heard was a VC warning to their own that a trail was mined. Lastly, it had just rained and there were little circular pools of rainwater spread along the trail, too perfect to be anything but man-made.

I raised my right hand (You never spoke while on patrol. Unlike all of the movies you've seen, noise is the absolute enemy of patrolling.), and SSgt D came up to me and said—"what?"

I pointed out the features of the trail ahead of me and said, "It looks mined."

He said, "Oh Bulls__t, Lindsey" and stepped onto the trail ahead of me.

There was an immediate explosion and SSgt D's left foot was completely blown off, up to the middle of his calf.

We hit the ground instantaneously and I saw black sharpened iron stakes in the brush in front of my face and I held up just short of hitting them. We tied off D's stump while he quietly grunted and said, "now I can't join the army and make rank." We gathered up his gear and his weapon, a brand-new M-79 40mm grenade launcher and at D's urging, moved back to the rice paddy behind us and a 3-foot-deep irrigation trench for cover.

SSgt D said: "They're coming. Fire one shot every few seconds but conserve ammo."

In seconds, the brush in front of us exploded in gunfire – ours and theirs – and we lay down in the brown stinking water of the trench to pop up and fire and then get back down into cover. I fired my M-14 and spotted someone behind a concrete gravestone to my right front and shot at the center of that stone and the shape fell behind it. Grenades were thrown and that trench protected us and nobody except SSgt D was injured. I had picked up SSgt D's M79 grenade launcher and ammunition and stuck my head and shoulders above that trench for what seemed to be an eternity, while I aimed it, fired and then watched where the round went, so I could aim the next one better. My first rounds went way over where I was aiming because I had overestimated the range but eventually, I started hitting where I wanted to. I used up all of his ammunition and then returned to firing my rifle. Cpl. A had trouble with his rifle and had to lie on his back in that trench and kick the bolt open for each shot, giving him the rate of fire of a Civil War musket.

A Marine rifle company showed up to our left and the fight ended abruptly. We evacuated D by the first helicopter that arrived (after it, an army Huey, tried to strafe us with its M-60 machine guns but missed) and tired, deaf from the noise, and nearly out of ammunition, returned to the battery. From that experience I learned to never, ever again come close to running out of ammunition.

The author, returning from that patrol, with 7 rounds left in the last magazine. (Photo from the Author's Collection)

Some years later, when I worked as a Fabrication Helper for Lockheed Aircraft Company in Burbank California, several of my co-workers asked me to tell a war story about my time in Vietnam, so I told them about us and SSgt D and that day's firefight. My fellow workers didn't believe me and accused me of "reading too many comic books." I was startled by their reactions and hurt, and I resolved never to tell any damn war story to people outside my fellow veterans again.

That same evening, as I left for "Dinner Break" – a half hour in the evening for Swing Shift – and as I was sadly heading out to get some food, I noticed that the uniformed guard on that gate had military creases on his grey shirt. Then I read his name tag and it said: "D___." I asked him if he was SSgt D of Bravo 1/11 and he said, "what's it to you?" (Still charming.) I told him that I was there, on the day he lost his foot. He brightened up and hoisted his pant leg up to show me his plastic foot – and at that exact moment, the crew that worked with me on that machine showed up and I said, "here's D – you go ahead and call him a liar!"

Like I said before – God has a great sense of humor, and a precise aim.

Our shot-down UH-34D in the battery position. A week after it force-landed, the Air Wing brought in an engine stand and a new engine, installed the engine and flew it back out of our position for home. (Photo by Ramon R. Alba, used with permission)

In September, we had a Helicopter crash-land in our battery position. We heard it coming, a Sikorsky UH-34D, its engine was misfiring, and it was trailing smoke, but it made a perfect landing just behind the gunline – missing all of the tent ropes, antennas, and barbed wire in our cramped position. The crew jumped out of the helicopter as soon as it stopped, one of the crew had orange smoke pouring from his belt: a smoke marker had been hit or just fired off while they were coming down. We ran a large fire extinguisher to the helicopter to put out any fire, but the engine didn't burn. Then we heard a long burst of gunfire arrive into our position from the same direction the helicopter came from.

The enemy force that had shot down that helicopter came out of the tree line about 600m to our southeast, dozens of them and we could see their green uniforms. I ran to Gun 5 (second from the left) and only had to turn the 105 a little bit to bring it to bear on the enemy. They were firing while advancing and they had to be from somewhere else because they were attacking the front of an artillery position in broad daylight. They appeared to be coming to finish off the helicopter, since we were almost invisible from their view, on the brow of the short hill we were living on. Cpl. A and one other Marine broke out High Explosive (HE) ammunition, and I called the XO Pit to get permission to open fire. I didn't get any answer and the enemy was still moving towards us and firing, maybe a third of the way or about 400 meters from us. Cpl. A and I made the decision to fire (I don't know where Gun 5's Section Chief, Sgt A was). I sighted the gun by looking down the barrel through the open breech (we didn't have a direct fire sight); then Cpl. A loaded a High Explosive round, Charge 7 (max charge), point detonating fuze. I pulled the lanyard and the round hit the ground in front of the enemy and ricocheted steeply upward and detonated maybe half a mile behind them, high in the air.

The fire in our direction increased, with some rounds hitting nearby. Cpl. A recommended decreasing the charge and using a time fuze. We fired another round and this time it went off behind them a couple of hundred meters. Cpl. A cut the fuze setting back further (Time: 2.0 seconds), and we reduced the charge to Charge 2 (almost the minimum possible) and this time the round went off right in the middle of them. I could see the sparks of the fragments hitting the ground. We kept firing – I think we fired at least 30 rounds – and then Gun #6 started firing too. We called out our firing data to them to help them get on target. Unbelievably, one of the helicopter crew members made it to our gun while we were firing and offered to buy a souvenir Chinese SKS rifle that I had slung across my back, and I told him to "wait until the fight's over!"

Cpl A (L), Me (Center) and PFC B (R) with the howitzer behind us and a pile of fired cases that day. The tree line the enemy came from is behind us. (Photo from the Author's Collection)

The enemy's attack stopped completely about 300 meters away and we kept firing. An ONTOS – a Marine-unique antitank vehicle with six 106mm recoilless rifles (see Appendix 1), pulled up to the left of Gun 6 and we knew what was coming next: the damn thing fired all six barrels at once, making an earth-shattering all-enveloping blast and obliterating the ground where we last saw the enemy and that was the end of that. The survivors ran back to the tree line and escaped. According to what we were told, they found about 20 dead and a lot of blood trails (implying that several more enemy had been wounded or killed and dragged off).

The infantrymen in our position normally slept most of the day but the sounds of all of the fighting woke them up and they came up to our gunline but by the time they got there, it was over. They were upset that we hadn't allowed the enemy to get closer so they could "kill all of them."

Then we heard shots from the rear – the northern side of our position. A couple of snipers were joining in the fight from about 300 meters, and they faced over 40 of our fully-roused grunts plus another ONTOS, and the gunfire was absolutely intense. You could see hits all over the rice paddies because they were flooded and then one after another, the snipers lost their nerve and ran. They were cut down by dozens of hits before they got very far. One of those running VC was killed by the ONTOS, firing just his .50 caliber spotting rifle.

A lieutenant led a squad to recover any intelligence information they could find on the enemy bodies in front of our position and then as it got dark, set up an L-shaped ambush over the bodies to catch anyone who might try to recover them. At some point, after it was really dark, the team heard voices coming and even saw someone smoking a cigarette. The team got ready to set off a Claymore mine to initiate the ambush until the lieutenant heard the word "f__k" spoken by the approaching men and had everyone hold their fire. He said, "Who goes there?" and the men coming said: "Who the f_ck wants to know?"

They brought the five men to our position where we discovered that they were navy destroyer sailors whose ship was docked in Danang. They had hitched a ride south on the main road and dropped off from their ride when they heard our firefight. They came toward us to watch and take pictures with a 35mm camera they were carrying but it got dark. Incredibly, they had walked smoking and making noise through a very dangerous area and blundered right into our ambush site. They were wearing Marine-type green utilities, a Marine style cover (hat) with the rear of them sewn to make them fit their heads and the bills were bent upward in some sort of goofy sailor style. They were completely unarmed except for a small hunting knife. They were mouthy and annoying and had no idea at all how close they came to a violent death. We took them back to Danang in the morning. Lieutenant O was disgusted with them and said, "What's this war coming to now? Tourists!"

The really bizarre part of this last story is that no record exists in the official Marine Corps records that I can find, except for the bare fact that the helicopter force-landed in our position, not in any of the unit diaries, command chronologies, nothing. It seems like this would be a great event for the Corps to have in the record but there is nothing but the slightest mention. This isn't the only time that I discovered that official records missed something that I clearly remember but it is the most surprising. When you know that the folks recording these events were usually sitting in a tent somewhere, or in the case of our battery, in a below-ground bunker and recording the day-to-day minutia on a manual typewriter, I guess there would be shortcuts taken – or maybe potentially embarrassing events deleted.

The air wing brought in a new engine and an engine stand for lifting it, the mechanics installed the new engine, and the helicopter flew home after just a few days after.

At around this time, late September 1966, Lt. O picked me to move to XO Pit to replace another Marine as the Battery Recorder. The XO Pit was the center of activity in the howitzer batteries and the Battery Recorder was the guy who spoke on the phones to the Section Chiefs on each gun to relay the firing data. I had a headset and microphone and we had wire lines going to all the guns in a loop. I had a recording sheet in front of me on a desk we made of empty ammunition boxes and as the data was calculated in the tent behind us, the Fire Direction Center I would receive it, write it on the recording sheet (The "Record of Firing Data") and then relay that data to the gun for use.

It would go like this:

I would hear "Battery Adjust, Action Front" over the headset and then push a button that rang an electric bell in the six gun tents. I would also pick up a bullhorn and yell: "Battery Adjust, Action Front"; so all the crews were alerted and running to their guns.

The Section Chiefs would check in over the phone line and I would pass the firing data:

"Gun 3 Adjust" (Meaning that Gun #3 would be aiming and firing first for the Forward Observer with the infantry)

"Deflection 2646, Shell HE, Charge 7, Fuze Quick (The direction for aiming, the shell is High Explosive, the charge is the maximum, and the fuze was point detonating, the most common type)

"Quadrant 346" (the elevation for the barrel)

Once Gun #3 reported "Gun Three Safe and Ready," the howitzer had all the proper aiming data applied and the loaded round was in the chamber, waiting for the command to fire.

I would turn to the XO and say—"Gun 3 is safe and ready," and he would stand in view of the gun crew, raise his hand high and yell: "Stannnnd Byyyye – FIRE!" and drop his hand and the gun was fired.

This process was repeated over and over until the Forward Observer had adjusted Gun 3's impacts onto his target and then the whole battery was fired.

It was an important job for me, and I applied myself doing it. I learned a great deal about the process and listening to the Conduct of Fire net on the radio we had in the XO Pit helped me to understand what the FO was asking for and sometimes it also told me about the urgency from the tone of the FO's voice and the sounds of rapid gunfire in the background. Lt O was easy to work for and I lived in the side portion of the XO Pit. My duties included cleaning and verifying the optics used to align the guns each morning and one morning just as it got light, I pulled the poncho off of the Aiming Circle (an instrument like a surveyor's transit) when a large cobra reared up underneath. I had my rifle ready but didn't know whether I should shoot or not, since I was in the center of a small hilltop with 120 or so artillerymen, 60 Engineers, and about 120 infantrymen. I saw Capt. C in his green underwear standing in front of his tent, so I yelled "what do I do?" and he yelled back: "Shoot it, you dumb sonofabitch!"

So, I shot the snake – and luckily didn't kill anyone else in our position.

Decades later, when Capt. C had retired as a judge in his second career and was reminded of our "morning cobra" he remembered that he had spotted the snake first and said, "Lance corporal, shoot the snake."

Nah. My version's correct – my memory's better.

Another memory of that time isn't fun to remember, it's the gunfight that killed PFC H. PFC H was a member of one of the gun sections who all of us liked. Then one day he began to cry and break all of his most cherished possessions. He took a hammer and smashed his expensive camera, his reel-to-reel tape player while we begged him not to. We offered to buy them from him, but he ignored us and kept crying and destroyed everything.

Later that evening after it was dark, H shot it out with two new guys who had just arrived at the battery and from what we later heard, those two were from the South and had called PFC H a racist name. H was killed and one of the two new guys was wounded in a gunfight at the outpost. We really liked H and it hit us hard to lose him – particularly to something as pointless as this. All he had to do was talk to us about those two guys and we could've handled them and their stupid mouths but arguments with rifles never come out well.

One evening when it was my turn on outpost, I saw about 40 villagers stealing lumber and sacks of concrete from the engineer's bridge work site to our southeast. They were taking advantage of the last bits of daylight – and the engineer's absence – to take as much material as they could, likely to use to build their family bunkers in their homes. It was understandable, but if the engineers were ever going to finish their bridge, they needed to keep their building supplies in place. The engineers couldn't leave security on the site at night because of the danger in that area; as the nearest American unit, we were stuck with keeping an eye on it. I called for Lt. O and when he came to my OP, he told me to fire a high burst of machine gun fire to get their attention. My machine gun had a Traverse and Elevation (T&E) on it, so it could be accurately adjusted. I cranked up the elevation well above them and fired a burst. Chut–chut-chut-chut and a stream of red tracers arced in the air high over the villagers, and they stopped, frozen where they were. Then I fired another burst, and they took all of the material back to the work site and stacked it where it had been. We were never going to actually shoot civilians for stealing – they were poor, and they looked at us as a wonderful source of goodies, but they got the message and we kept our stuff, this time.

THE PX

We were allowed to go the 16 km north to Danang to the Post Exchange (PX) occasionally to buy things. It was located right next to a slum portion of Danang we called "Dogpatch." There really wasn't very much to buy there, but it was something to do and beat sitting around the battery on working parties. The PX itself was a large Butler Building – a metal prefab warehouse – and it was guarded by an MP at the door. We used to annoy the MP on duty by refusing to unload our rifles when we went in. We'd tell him: "Son, this thing's been loaded longer than you've been in country" and breeze by him. I'm sure that we were scary with our torn and bleached out utilities with holes in the knees and faded flak vests and our apparent readiness to go nuts.

We resented that MP because he had clean, pressed utilities and highly polished boots and he was shiny clean, well-shaven, and safe. His presence also implied that we were the danger, not the enemy. We kept our weapons loaded at all times. Not really to defy the well-washed and shiny MPs but because the enemy could show up at any time, any place and only an idiot would trust his life to an unloaded weapon.

Like I said there wasn't much to buy in the PX: shaving gear, soap, cigarettes, maybe tropical chocolate (which had a gritty and obnoxious texture), sometimes cameras, most of the time weeks-old issues of *Time* and *Newsweek* magazines printed on tissue-thin paper and sometimes, issues of the *Star and Stripes* military newspaper which really gave us the best information of all.

The "Rear area" around Danang had the airfield people, the supply personnel, the ammo and fuel dump types, and a lot of mechanics and other technicians to keep our machines running and the supplies coming. It was joked at the time that we were "the first Dragon that was 10% teeth and 90% tail" and that was true enough, Yet, conducting a major war 10,000 miles from home couldn't happen without the "REMFs" (Rear Echelon M_____f____ers) hanging around in brand-new stuff in Danang and elsewhere. I think that we resented them because they were as safe as anyone could be in Vietnam – and good food, clean beds, and showers – yet they would go back home and be "war veterans." The other thing that rankled was that they had all the new stuff—the new Jungle Utilities, the Jungle Boots and brand-new everything and very little trickled out to us in the field. The first pair of Jungle Boots I got were from a pile of them with other men's names on them, taken from the dead. All of our uniforms were ragged and getting socks and underwear was usually done by writing to our parents at home, having them go to a Surplus Store in the States, buy them, and then send them to us in the mail. Most of that good gear (and food and beer) seemed to have been stalled in the plush rear and didn't reach men doing the shooting. Some of that may have been lousy Supply Officers at our end but we tended to blame the rear area commandos for siphoning things off.

Close to December I saw a sight that startled me at the Danang PX: we were waiting in line for another visit to the hot, empty store when a van pulled up and four army colonels armed with M3 "Greasegun" submachineguns got out, looking all tense and ferocious (and a bit overweight), looking primarily at us. Then a young blonde woman got out of the van wearing a very short skirt and a lot of makeup. The four colonels formed a cordon around her as she smiled happily, and they walked her past our line into the PX. The van had her name painted on the side and apparently, she was some sort of celebrity on the Armed Force Radio and TV System and since none of us had radios or TV, we'd never heard of her. We must have been some pretty dangerous dudes to need four (4) O-6s with submachine guns to protect her from us! It seemed to add an almost cartoonish angle to an already ridiculous side of our war. Like, what in heaven's name was an armed forces Radio and TV system needed for in a war, anyway?

By this time, I was an established member of our battery and most of the early arrivals had rotated back home, their 13 months complete. I also indulged in a bit of "gunsmithing" with my M-14 to improve its performance for me: I used fine stones I borrowed from the armory to hone the contact surfaces of the sear and hammer hooks to lighten and smooth the trigger pull and I cut one coil from the hammer spring to further lighten the trigger. I installed a full-auto selector kit and experimented with a small slab of rubber as a buffer to slow the rate of fire from 800 rounds per minute to something more controllable. I placed the sling around the wrist of the stock and extended it using a blanket roll strap, so it could be carried muzzle forward comfortably and swung quickly to either side. My rifle became "my own" and I was very skilled at using it at any range.

Despite our work bring medical assistance to the village complex near us, Vietcong activities increased and the sniper fire suddenly improved. Our old "duty sniper" would fire one shot in our direction but very high and so regularly that we could set our watches by him – 4:00 every day. Since he never came close, we didn't bother shooting back at him.

One day the enemy replaced him with someone a lot more serious and a Gunnery Sergeant with our combat engineer platoon was killed and several of the guys had near misses (including one administrative clerk who stuck his head out of the entrance out of the admin bunker like a ground hog and got hit through the ear). I remember how heavy that dead Gunny felt when we carried him on a stretcher.

The battery position, with the gunline to the right rear, the Admin Bunker in the foreground, and the rows of pallets for walking once the rain started. (Photo by Ramon R. Alba, used with permission)

"Fort Bravo" battery position – Hill 55 to right top, main North-South road to left. This aerial photo was taken while Bravo was out of the position and the gunline is occupied by M109 self-propelled howitzers. The Gun Tents are the row of six tents in the center, the Fire Direction Center is just back of the Gun Tents in the center, and the Mess Hall and the Armory are at center left in the photo. The row of empty spaces for tents were where our infantry company used to live and the small dots around the perimeter were our security bunkers for our Outposts. (Photo from the Author's Collection)

Capt C (L), Lt O (M), Sgt A(R). They were our leaders, our parents, and the only people who presumably knew what was really going on. (Photo by Ramon R. Alba, used with permission)

Capt. C ordered Gun 1 (farthest to the right) to return fire at the sniper with 105mm high explosive and they fired several rounds directly into the tree line where we thought he was. Don't think we got him but should have scared him a bit.

Another day we saw a Navy F-8 Crusader fighter on fire, heading north across us on a path to Danang airfield. As we watched, the plane exploded into bits and the first thought was that the pilot had been killed. Then we saw a parachute open, and the pilot drifted slowly down, heading right for the section of the tree line where we got the most enemy activity, and you could hear shots being fired at him.

Improbably, Capt. C looked at me and said, "what should we do?" I told him that we should grab anyone that has a rifle and ammunition to come to the XO Pit now and we'd take a truck as close as we could get and rescue the pilot.

He said, "do it" and I took the bullhorn and called everyone with a weapon and ammo on him as I recommended. When we had 12-13 armed Marines, I started the truck, drove it out of our position and around our barbed wire perimeter and out into the rice paddies. I got about 200m or halfway across the paddies when the front of the truck sank in the mud, we jumped out and ran as fast as we could through mid-thigh deep mud and water until we got to the edge of the tree line. I was so out of breath that I couldn't even pull the trigger of my rifle when two VC ran right across my front, no more than 25 yards away. The Marines to my right found the pilot hiding behind a haystack and we got him back to our position.

It was too late in the afternoon by then to drive him to Danang, so he stayed in our position that night. We showed him movies on the side of a tent (the TV shows *Batman* and *Combat* – we never got first-run or even second-run movies, just goofy black and white TV shows) and listened to him tell us about his experiences as a pilot, hitting North Vietnamese targets.

Even though I was now the Battery recorder, it didn't exempt me from the many menial duties of a Lance Corporal. I still unloaded artillery ammunition from trucks, stood outpost duty at night, and occasionally, tower watch. We had a short 15 foot "tower" in the center of our position that had a sandbag wall around it and a roof made of a poncho. It also had a BC Scope (Battery Commander's Telescope: a periscope-like instrument that allowed you to accurately and safely view from behind the sandbags) and we were expected to continuously scan the tree lines around us while we were on duty.

Most of the time, my fellow Marines used the time on tower watch to read racy magazines, but I actually did watch carefully when it was my turn. One of those days, a sniper shot at me closely enough to hit the poncho inches above my head. I looked carefully through the BC scope, traversing slowly – and then spotted a face looking straight at me from behind a small berm in front of the far tree line about 500m away. I grabbed my rifle and set my sights for that range. But being the guy I was, I cranked up my phone and called the XO Pit to tell them that I saw the sniper and I was going to fire. Lt. O told me to wait, and he'd be right up. He scrambled up the ladder and got behind the scope and he easily spotted him too.

He said, "give me your rifle." I objected because I knew that I could hit the guy but when the Lieutenant insists, you hand your rifle over. He took a long and careful aim while I watched through the BC scope and he missed by maybe 6 feet to the left. I saw the VC and another man with him, and they got away running.

Lt. O never said a word. I think we both knew that there would have been a better chance that I would have gotten him if I had been shooting.

There was a road to the left front (South East) of our position at "Fort Bravo" that used to be a railway bed and it branched to our pontoon bridge and then onto a road called Anderson Trail that led to the 1st Marines position to the South and East of Hill 55. The part of that road that traversed the left front was partially concealed by a grove of trees and each night a Vietcong team emplaced a large mine in that road and each morning, an engineer team went out to find the mine, disarm it and open the road to the day's traffic. The engineer team was led by a few infantrymen, followed by two engineers with mine detectors, sweeping from side to side, an M274 Mechanical Mule with additional engineers, a jeep following them, and then an M48 tank. One morning the VC apparently forgot about the tank and decided to ambush the engineer team. We heard the gunfire and looked up to see a jeep racing down the road towards us, with wounded men slumped in it. Immediately after, we heard tank fire thundering first towards us and then away from us as they fired canister rounds (tank shells that contained 1,281 steel balls, like buckshot from a huge shotgun) at the ambushers on both sides of the road. The tank emerged from the cover of the trees and its turret traversed slowly, looking for any sign of the VC. It was pretty clear that the tank was the deciding factor in that ambush. Sometime later there was a huge explosion and flame from that road in the middle of the night and a large crater was left in the road in the morning. It was obvious that the VC mining team screwed up and vaporized themselves while putting in their nightly mine.

Sometime later, I drove down that road and onto Anderson Trail to bring two new Lieutenants to the 1st Marines so they could start their duty as Forward Observers and while were just a bit past the bridge, we started to take fire. One of the Lieutenants, Lt H, objected to how fast I was going until I pointed out the new bullet holes in our jeep. I believe that he told me to "go faster" after he saw the hits on us. (An astute reader will note that my military driver's license was torn up a while before. It turns out that I "didn't need that stinking license" – it's Vietnam for gosh sakes!)

Me, and my "stolen" jeep. I got that jeep from the Navy while I was in Danang on a PX run. I found a Trip Ticket blowing along on the road, so I took that to the Dispatcher at the navy motor pool a few yards away and the sailor on duty handed me the keys to unlock the steering wheel on this jeep. I took this as a sign that we should have that jeep and so I drove the jeep to our position and gave it a yellow USMC number and stenciled our tactical markings and voilá, we had a new jeep. Hopefully, the Statute of Limitations has expired for Grand Theft, Jeep. Note the Batman emblem on the front of my helmet and just visible were my Medevac number (LFR 7173) and my blood type. On the back, in large letters, I had "The Indispensable Lindsey." So much for humility. (Photo from the Author's Collection)

We had nearly endless fire missions during September and October 1966 and during that same time the monsoons continued, and the rain never seemed to stop. The lower ground, the paddies and around them, filled up with water and the area became a huge lake and we became an island. The much-reduced patrolling was done in rubber boats and all kinds of reptiles, rats and insects came up to share our hilltop. Anything we had made of fabric or paper or leather almost rotted while we watched. Family pictures lost their surface emulsion, and rust, mud and mold were everywhere. The mood became perceptibly lower, and the rain wasn't the only cause.

Lt. O summoned some of us to the XO Pit and told us to build a bulletin board from ammunition box wood and to paint it red. It sounded crazy but who were we to object? We built it, then he told us to mount it right in the middle of the position. We began to wonder what was happening to our XO's mind, but we did as we were told.

Next, he called for a formation by the bulletin board – more insanity: we were clustered together in neat rows in "sniper alley." As we stood there, nervously waiting for the shots to hit, Lt. O told us that he had heard that a number of us had received "Dear John" letters from our sweethearts at home and that he himself had a gotten a Dear John from his wife. He said that he was ordering us to post all of our Dear John letters on that bulletin board so everyone could read them, and he said that he was going to start with his own – and he thumbtacked his wife's letter to the top left of the board.

Within a few hours, both sides of that board were covered with letters. It turned out that the majority of the men of our battery (including me – though I was happy to get mine; now she was somebody else's problem) had been dumped and we discovered that all of the letters seemed to be alike, same format and almost the same wording with only the names changed. Everybody laughed at each other's letters and the mood perceptibly improved.

The sun yellowed the paper, the rain made the ink run and one by one, the letters blew off in the wind.

It was only sometime later that we discovered that Lt. O wrote his own Dear John letter and he's still married to his lovely wife.

I became more and more proficient at my job as a Recorder, and I was able to pick out on a map where the target was going to be by listening to the FO's call for fire and I was able to get the crews on the guns and part of the data already ready by the time that FDC was ready to send it.

One evening, we had an unknown American voice on the radio asking for help. After asking some questions of the man on the radio, we were able to establish that it was an Air Force NCO in a crashed rescue helicopter somewhere to the south of us in very bad territory. He did not know where they were, but the rest of the crew were injured, and they had only one machine gun to defend themselves. Lt O worked up some probable locations based on the direction of the setting sun from the crew and their view of prominent mountains around them. Lt O told them to watch for an illumination round fired above them and to tell us where they saw it.

We fired at fairly long range for us, and the NCO told us in what direction the light of the flare was to him. Lt O worked up another target to shoot and we fired another illumination round. The NCO spotted it and reported his direction to it. We had them pinpointed now and we fired one more round calculated to go off right above them and it did.

The enemy had started shooting at that crew and we could hear the gunfire on the radio. Lt O plotted six separate targets in a circle around their crash site but far enough away from them to have a healthy safety margin and each gun fired in turn at their point on the circle. The Air Force NCO – a highly competent guy and amazingly calm – helped us refine the targets to be exactly where they needed to be.

Then each time that NCO told us that the enemy was approaching, we fired High Explosive in that circle around them and we kept it up all night. We had everyone breaking out ammunition, full time and we started sending trucks to Danang, lights on, to the main ammunition dump and back. Every time the enemy started to pick up the rate of fire at the plane crew, we intensified the artillery fire to protect them.

At dawn, we stopped hearing from them but soon an Air Force helicopter flew over our position and men were waving at us and we waved back. A minute or so later, two USAF F-4 Phantoms flew towards us, inverted, and the pilots saluted.

We had a mess to clean up and cannons to re-barrel – we had burned out some of the barrels that night – but we had a deep satisfaction for what we had done.

Another night later, I heard an emergency fire mission coming through the radio. The enemy was close to overrunning a unit in the field and the intensity of fire made it hard to hear the FO's voice. I got the battery ready as always and then realized that Lt. O was still asleep. I tried to wake him, but he didn't respond. (He wasn't a drinker, so it wasn't alcohol.)

Because it was an emergency and lives depended on us, I told the Section Chiefs that I was having trouble waking Lt. O and that I would fire the battery. The Section Chiefs told me that there was no way that they would fire on the word of Lance Corporal and that they would refuse to shoot.

I tried to wake the XO again, even picking the head end of his cot up and dropping it – but nothing. I heard the desperation on the radio and since it was absolutely dark and nobody could see the XO Pit, I told the section chiefs—"OK, the XO is here!"—and then I dropped my voice to a lower pitch and yelled over the bullhorn "Batteryyy, Stannnd byyyye, – FIRE!" And they did fire, raggedly, and I threw in "Get it together, Girls!"

Then Lt O woke up. I had a lot of explaining to do.

As I said a little earlier, I was still required to stand outpost duty – as well as tower watch duty and security patrols. There were twelve outposts around our battery perimeter, just within the double rows of concertina barbed wire. Each outpost was a bunker and mortar hole: the bunker to shelter us and protect a machine gun position and the mortar hole to get into during a mortar attack. Usually, we stayed outside of the bunker and walked around near it, partially to keep awake and partially because visibility was so restricted when you were inside. One of the features of life in Vietnam was the distinctive and ubiquitous 81mm illumination rounds fired from mortars almost all the time. They were fired almost every minute from positions near us to keep the area lit up to allow us to see the enemy around us. The first part you saw was the small flash high above as the round expelled its magnesium "candle" and parachute and then the larger flash as the candle ignited in brilliant white light high above us and its parachute slowly descended. Then you'd hear the "poom" sound from the round opening and then a high-pitched whistling "whoop, whoop, whoop" sound as the now-empty rear part of the round tumbled downward to the ground. All night long – "poom" and then "whoop, whoop, whoop" – every night for as long as we were in Vietnam. It was a constant, pervasive element in our lives and yet I haven't seen even one movie about our war in Vietnam that featured the sounds of the mortar illumination rounds.

Day after day, I watched the infantry company that was sharing our position load up for combat, go out of our wire and head across the rice paddies to face the enemy in the tree lines. There would be a few shots at first, then an overwhelming, stuttering roar of thousands of shots fired, the regular crump of grenades and green and red tracers lacing through the air above them. Next, we'd see the colored smoke behind the trees and the medevacs started.

I felt guilty. I knew that even though I was in an important supporting role, I also knew that the infantry – the grunts – were taking the main risks. I knew that I had some skills that I had accumulated through my 11 months of experience, and I felt that it would be stupid to replace me with some new Marine who had to learn everything from scratch. I also knew that I didn't have anybody waiting for me at home, so I had less to lose.

I decided in November 1966 that I would extend my time in Vietnam by another six months and requested to be assigned as a Forward Observer and take my portion of the risks with the infantry.

Just as I made my request, I was finally selected for R&R and the only location available to me was Taipei, Taiwan.

R &R

"REST AND RECREATION." R&R WAS AN INTERESTING FEATURE
of our war. It was a really organized and elaborate US-sponsored prostitution
in foreign countries. No point in sugar-coating it. I have never found the
origins of this system, but the idea was to take all of us at some mid-point of
our time in Vietnam to another country; likely with the idea that it would re-
strain us from getting in trouble in Vietnam with the locals. The countries and
locations in question were apparently fine with it and provided all the facilities
and support and young women to support this system. The choices (if you
were influential enough to have a choice) were: Tokyo, Japan, Bangkok, Thai-
land, Manila, The Philippines, Taipei, Taiwan, and Kuala Lumpur, Malaysia.
Officers could pick Hawaii to meet up with their wives or Sydney, Australia,
where one would assume, they wouldn't be meeting their wives.

We bottom-ranking types got what we were given.

I considered myself to be a good, moral kid – but when my quota came
up, I just went with it. I got a ride from the battery position to the Danang
airfield, dressed in a khaki uniform but I kept my rifle. When I got to Danang,
I was put into a barracks tent with other Marines waiting for the morning R&R
flights. I didn't know any of them, but we got along well. Soon after I picked
a cot and stowed my gear, I was invited to join a card game in progress, but I
begged off, telling them that I didn't gamble. They kept trying to get me to
play, so I said that I would – but only one hand: that no matter what I won or
lost, I would play that hand and quit. They agreed. It was five card stud, and I
won my hand, taking $600 in winnings (about $4,200 in today's money). They
weren't happy with me but stuck to our agreement and I kept the money.

The Author, all cleaned up and ready for R&R, November 1966. (Photo from the Author's Collection)

Since our flights didn't leave until morning, one of the guys suggested going to the Air Force side of the base and go to their Enlisted Club and get some beer. It was raining heavily, so we slogged across the runway to that Air Force Club and knocked on the door, soaking wet and heavily armed. A large NCO bouncer answered the door and told us that "Marines aren't allowed." We kept trying to convince him that all we wanted was one beer and soon a chorus of voices in the club were yelling "let them in"; so eventually and begrudgingly he let us four in.

The beer, which was something we hadn't had for a while, began to have effect fast and we got rowdy. Arguments started – with some airmen against us and some airmen on our side and things got noisier while the big bouncer glared at us. Then one of our number slapped a Vietnamese waitress across the bottom with a wet hat while she was bent over taking an order and she went tottering into someone's lap and they both fell on the floor. Then all hell broke loose, fists flying and glass breaking. We had some Air Force guys fighting us and some Air Force guys who had become "honorary Marines" fighting on our side. The bouncer got knocked out with a rifle butt and mirrors were broken and paneling torn down. After a short period, we heard vehicles outside and figured it was time to leave, so we left out of a side window and ran to the base theater (the Air Force had it good) and pretended to be watching a movie when the MPs arrived. As I understand it, after that Marines were permanently banned from the Air Force side of the base. They might be still looking for us; the Air Force never forgives or forgets.

In the morning, I boarded an even-then ancient DC-6 prop airliner and flew to Taipei. I was met at the airport by a young Chinese guy who called himself "Mike" who had a blue 1961 Chevrolet and he drove me downtown for the first order of business, to buy suitable clothing. I was expertly fitted with suits and pants and shirts – and remember I was wealthy – I bought a lot, and everyone was very pleased. Next, I got a hotel room in a nice hotel that had the name of "Palace" something or other. By this time, it was late at night, so I thought we were done. Nope, next we went to a bar, and I was introduced to about four young women and told that I could pick anyone I wanted. They were all wearing those long and ornate silk Chinese dresses with high necks, and I was tired and a little buzzed, so I just picked one with the prettiest dress and we went to my hotel room for the night.

She called herself "Alice" and in the morning, we went and got breakfast, which was excellent Chinese food, of course, and we talked. She knew very little English, and I knew zero Chinese, so we kept it simple. She said she was a farmer's daughter, and she was hoping to earn enough money to buy her own farm when she was done with her current job and marry somebody worthwhile. Her work didn't seem to have much stigma with her fellow citizens, and we were greeted by families and everyone with warmth when we were in public. I spent lavishly (since, as I mentioned before, thanks to my card game, I was "rich") and bought her clothes and jewelry at a modern department store. Taipei was clean, modern, beautiful, and very friendly. We took a tour to the mountains and visited and danced with the aboriginal people there, called the Wu Lai and rode a long and fragile-looking rail line that wound around the tall peaks. The weather was perfect and the company enjoyable and since I was a generous spender, some of Alice's girlfriends joined us and I bought clothes for them too – after all, I believed, I didn't have long left to live anyway.

On the last evening left in Taipei, I took Alice and her friends to an expensive restaurant which had a large stage that could rotate and elevate as needed. I remember the main act being Chinese acrobats who were very skilled and beautifully costumed. A prosperous-looking man at a table near me with a large family called to me and asked if the girls at my table were "all yours?"

I nodded without really understanding his drift and he stood – and the rest of the people in the restaurant stood – and they all applauded. Grateful for my boost to the local economy, I guess.

I should be ashamed to tell anyone that I spent those five days on R&R, but it was part of the whole experience, and it was huge boost to my spirits to spend those days with someone completely unconnected to our war, in a safe and exotic environment. I guess that was what R&R was for. Alice even sent me a letter a couple of months later, but I couldn't find anyone who could read the Chinese for me.

I had turned 21 while I was on R&R and hardly noticed it.

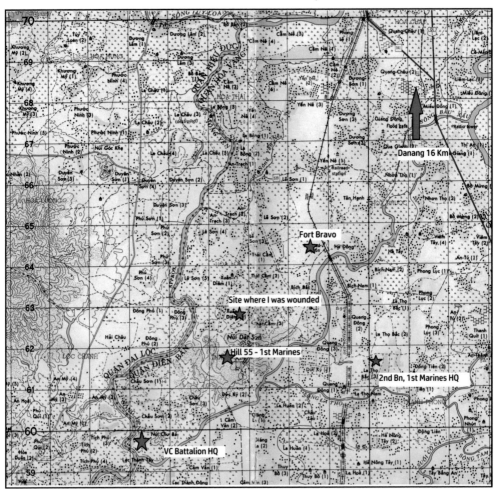

Map of our sector, South and West of Danang, "Indian Country" or "Dodge City," depending on who you ask. Each square on the map is one kilometer. Note that the VC Battalion Headquarters that we knew about was only 5 or 6 kilometers away from our battery position.

When I got back to Bravo battery, it had been mortared and our new CO, Captain W (our irreverent nickname for him was "Wilma") had been lightly wounded (according to the troops, he was trying to take pictures from his mortar hole and got nicked in the temple by fragments). Considering the accuracy of the attack – according to official records 14 rounds hit within the position but some troops claimed as many as 200 – rounds of 82mm mortar, it was miraculous that only two had been wounded and nobody had been killed. Part of that miracle was that one of the OPs (outposts) had spotted a vertical flash in the distance and properly read that as an enemy mortar firing and then started cranking our manually-operated siren. Everyone within the battery position dove into their pre-dug mortar holes and were safely below ground when the rounds arrived. However, every truck and tent and howitzer had received some damage. This had been part of a major coordinated attack against several artillery positions at once and our battalion headquarters. All had been accurately targeted simultaneously to keep us from interfering with their other attacks.

One of the trucks that had been hit worst by the mortar fire was shredded with so many holes it looked like a colander. Once the glass was replaced and new tires put on, it ran fine but whistled in in the wind when it was driven. The only parts of the body that didn't have a lot of holes were the door panels, so Cpl A was commissioned to paint something appropriate on each door. He painted a large Purple Heart Medal on both doors but instead of George Washington's face, he painted the grinning face of Alfred E. Neumann from *Mad Magazine*. It seemed to be a perfect emblem for our war.

Out with the Infantry

I HAD PUT MY REQUEST IN FOR EXTENSION AND NEW DUTY, BUT LT. O tried his best to talk me out of it. He spent most of the night talking to me, arguing how dangerous it was and that "almost everyone who extends gets killed." I appreciated his concern, but I was determined to go ahead and do it. I believed that I had nothing to go back home to anyway and as I said before, better to have an experienced me than some new guy of uncertain talent.

After his attempt to get me to change my mind failed, he trained me to use a map, trained me on how to use the "Shackle" (grid position coding) system, taught me how to compose and send a fire mission and then walked me outside the battery about 1500 meters and had the battery fire for me into an open area.

Once that one-day training was done, I was driven to the headquarters of the 1st Marines and I was assigned to Echo Company 2nd Bn, 1st Marines as their new artillery scout. I'd love to say that the grunts were happy to see me, but they weren't. They were indifferent. My Forward Observer officer was Lt. D, a short southern officer who seemed to dislike me and his radio operator, Cpl B wasn't friendly either. I was sent to a GP tent to find a cot to sleep in but the only one available had a rip in the center and it slowly tore bit by bit all night until my butt was almost on the ground by morning.

In the morning we headed out on foot to positions along a river, looking for VC. I had the same familiar adrenaline rush when I loaded up and left the safe perimeter, but it was even more so now, knowing that I was finally with a grunt company, and we were heading for the real war.

About mid-morning we took some sniper fire from a house on the other side of a river and Lt. D told me to put together a fire mission to hit that house.

It was meant to be a test of my abilities, but it was also my first real fire mission. Everyone was watching as I carefully compared the map with the house's apparent position, wrote down all of the parts of the message and then gave it to Cpl. B to transmit. Lt. D asked me what I thought the grid (location) was and I told him and much to everyone's amusement he loudly disagreed. Nonetheless, the mission was sent and before long we had the message "On the way, Bravo" which meant that a round was fired from Bravo battery. I'd picked a smoke round because:

1. They were reasonably safe if you missed but showed where you had to "adjust" the next shot and
2. We had a lot of dense vegetation all around us and I wanted to see where the round landed – high explosive could get lost in the heavy stuff.

I heard the round go whiffling over and then heard a loud pop when it went off – but nothing was visible. Cpl. B was laughing theatrically and lying on his back, wiping the tears from his eyes. Lt. D said, "What now, Lindsey?"—also amused. So I said that I would change rounds to White Phosphorus and shoot again (since WP was much more visible). Just as I was saying this, plumes of white smoke began to pour out of the house's windows – by the purest luck, my lost round had gone through the roof of my target house. Lt. D wasn't any friendlier, but it shut Cpl. B up for a while. Lt D insisted that I carry a pistol since I was "now an FO." But it took only one firefight where I lay flat on the ground, helpless to shoot back at a tree line beyond the pistol's useful range to convince me that I needed my rifle back. Another good reason to carry a rifle was that snipers tried to pick off officers when they could and carrying a pistol was a good way to get shot.

During a long walk to another objective, I was reading our map, a French color map based on aerial photographs that we called a "Pictomap." I saw a tan colored "A" shape that was just over ridge from us and remarked to the ever-grumpy Lt. D that it looked like an airfield. As always, he disagreed and loudly made fun of "Lindsey's Airfield." Our battalion commander, LtCol H, heard him and walked over and told him to: "listen to your Lance Corporal – that's an old Japanese fighter strip the Japs used to protect their shipping during the war." Luckily for me Lt. D was sent to his next assignment. He wasn't fun to have around and there was no love lost when he and Cpl. B were gone.

The area around Hill 55 was largely deserted by the villagers so it was a safe bet that anyone you ran into was the enemy. Since Lt. D and Cpl. B had left for their next assignments and I was the FO (as full Lance Corporal of Marines) and I had my own radio operator, Cpl. R.

One day we were walking down a long, elevated road (again, that French railway bed) on a really hot day and the Marine in front of me started to sag and then stumbled down the slope to the right of the road. I was carrying what was a fairly light load as the FO, so I went down the hill after him. He was loaded with a backpack of mortar ammunition, and he was overheated so I poured some water on his head and took his pack off and put it on my back; then helped him to his feet and back up the hill. When I got up to the top again, the grunts were all smiles and started patting me on the back and saying, "Way to go Arty!" ("Arty" was a nickname applied to anybody that came from the artillery – saved having to actually know one's name). I made sure that from then on that I'd carry the same load as the infantry around me.

Around Christmas 1966, I went to the battery to take a class on the .50 caliber machinegun – I was finally going to learn how to use the darn thing – and they had four guns on tripods set up on the rear – south side – of Hill 55. We had been taking turns installing barrels, head spacing and timing them and then firing in short bursts to learn how to control the trigger and to avoid burning up the barrel.

During a break in the class, I was standing further up the slope from the class and was talking to Sgt. K, an infantry sergeant who had just attended church services. He told me that he had children at home and was due to go home soon. Then I heard a loud bang, very close to my right ear and I thought that my rifle had just gone off from its position slung on my right shoulder. I hit the ground hard as our instincts had driven us to learn and I saw that Sgt. K was dead, blood pouring from his neck and down under me.

A sniper in the tree line opposite us had shot Sgt. K, killing him while we were face to face and that bullet had narrowly missed me to hit him.

I never knew and still don't know why he died instead of me. I'll have to ask when I get to where I'm going.

The grunts were always active. Every single day was spent out in the field and patrolling, looking for the enemy. The biggest surprise I had was that <u>all</u>

of the grunts had been wounded. All of them! Some of them had wounds they wouldn't even report – they considered them insignificant – and most of the smaller wounds were from their own grenade fragments: the M-26 fragmentation grenade was so effective that you really couldn't throw the thing far enough to keep from being hurt by it. The grunts would pick out the bits of steel, smear on some antiseptic cream, bandage the hole, and then keep going. Many of them had been wounded the required three times to automatically go home, but they didn't report the minor stuff so they could stay with their unit. It was kind of a manliness thing. By my own analysis, the average time for a Marine rifleman to last before being seriously wounded or killed was about a month and half. Very few of them ever made it all the way through a full 13 months. Our Company Commander, Captain P, was an exceptional officer who made sure that everybody in the company knew exactly where we were going, the objectives of the operation, where to go if they got separated from the company, etc., etc. He was a really fine leader, and he conveyed a sincere concern for us and the Vietnamese. I stuck close to him and whenever he wanted a fire mission, I was right next to him to call it in. We used to kid each other about where we were. It's very easy to get disoriented in the heavy vegetation so FOs like me were used as "navigators" to keep an eye on where we were on our maps at any time. He would say that we were in one place, and I'd insist that no, we were someplace else, and the bets would fly (we had lots of completely worthless money so betting and card games were much-loved pastimes). I would call in a fire mission for an illumination round at a certain grid intersection. If Capt. P was right, the round should pop to our left. If I was right, then the round should pop to our right. The bets would go around for a while, then silence as we waited for the round to arrive. I was usually right, so my popularity with the bet winners grew. Captain P, God bless him, was a good sport and was fast with the praise when it went in my favor.

One of my favorite memories of Capt. P was when we were doing a company sweep through an almost completely deserted village in the middle of yet another smothering hot, humid day. We stopped to eat our C-Rations and the Skipper noticed an older farmer with one arm, struggling to plow his field behind a water buffalo. The house next to us had one corner on the ground and the farmer's wound looked fresh. He sent me and our *Chieu Hoi* (a former VC who had chosen to work for us under the "Open Arms" program) Dau, to ask what happened to him. We went out to him to talk to him, and he told us that an artillery round had hit next to the corner of his house, killing his wife and taking off the lower part of his arm. I asked him whose artillery round did it and he looked at me and said, "Does it make any difference?"

I reported what the farmer had said, and Capt P lowered his head and said, "I hate this war" and then called for the three platoon commanders to come in. He told them: "First platoon, you have security – nobody comes in around this farm. Second Platoon, you're going to plow a field and Third Platoon, we're rebuilding a house." He was one of the finest officers I ever knew.

One evening our company set up in a group of deserted houses for our evening perimeter and as always, I crawled out through the tall grass with my radio operator Cpl. R. to find an open spot to set up on-call targets for fast response during the night. I picked some likely-looking directions as possible avenues of approach and had the battery fire one round of smoke at each one to confirm the locations as targets. We had just gotten back into our perimeter (always a nervous thing when you're coming back into a circle of trigger-happy and excitable Marines) and within an hour or so of getting back, we were attacked from exactly the same direction that R and I had gone earlier. I called our battery asking for one of my pre-planned targets. As soon as the first round came in, I shifted the point of impact a bit to hit where the main mass of tracers was coming from and then had the battery fire three rounds in effect (which means the whole battery, all six guns, fire three rounds each rapidly for a total of 18 rounds fired). The attack was halted, and the enemy stopped shooting. In the morning, LtCol. H found out where I was and came out to compliment me on how well things went.

Another evening later, after it got dark, and a stream of tracers came rushing across the river at us – it seemed to be coming directly at me. I was relieving myself against a tree at the time and hit the deck so fast I landed in my own puddle. I returned fire with my M-14 rifle when a lieutenant nearby yelled for me to stop shooting my rifle and start calling in artillery. I quickly shifted one of my already-prepared targets over to the source of those tracers and started beating them up with High Explosives – as I should have been doing from the start.

Some have wondered why the infantry in Vietnam always patrolled in lines; it was very simple: since the vegetated areas were very difficult to traverse, we were often channelized through open spots and trails. The trails were often mined and of course, easily used for ambushes. To counter the restricted terrain, we were forced to move in long lines and to counter ambushes and the mines, we had to use experienced and skilled "point men" and parallel lines of Marines to the flanks of the main column. The Point man had to be a very sharp individual to spot mine triggers and tripwires while also sensing the presence of the enemy, hopefully before they detected us. A good point man was a very valuable guy and admired. It was also hideously dangerous, and we often lost point men almost as soon as they started. We could transition very quickly to attack formations when needed but most of the patrolling was in long lines. I remember watching a line of grunts, every other man carrying a white flare parachute in his pack (they were prized as insulating liners to our tents) looking like a long string of beads and since we were returning to our position, they were singing that goofy popular song of that time *They call it mellow yellow.*

We would often enter a village that had never seen Americans before and it would appear deserted at first. Then the kids, would appear and we'd give them the "S__it Discs" from our C-Rations and cigarettes (all the kids smoked). Then the old people would come out of hiding, and then after a while, everyone else. They saw that we were friendly and not wrecking anything and more or less generous with the smokes and the food. We'd ask them where the VC were, and they'd answer "không biêt" (I don't know} and we'd move on. We were pretty sure that they did know but they lived there and most likely some of their family were VC, so we didn't hold it against them. The next time we would go through that village, nobody bothered hiding and they'd give us pineapples or mangoes and sometimes even tell us where the mines were as we went through.

Sometimes we harvested our own mangoes by lying on our backs and firing our rifles at the topmost branches until a full branch loaded with ripe mangoes fell to us and we feasted.

One job I remember doing once was escorting a sniper who was assigned to us to his "hide position." He was an interesting character. All good humor and friendliness but he carried a Winchester Model 70 rifle in .30-06 with a long telescope and his work was killing at long range. I was assigned to cover his back, facing the opposite direction from him with my M-14, while he chose his target at first light and killed the guy. This guy never missed and specialized in shots through the neck. If his rifle fired, someone was dead.

His sidearm, in case we ran into something close up, was an ancient M1896 Mauser "Broomhandle" pistol that he carried in a shoulder holster. How he got it and how he managed to keep it was a mystery, but I know that he used captured Chinese ammunition to load it. That guy had style.

Early in my time as an artillery scout, I was picked to go into a tunnel to look for the enemy. I was picked because I was skinny and because I was still an outsider to the infantry company, and I had a .45 along with my rifle. I stripped off all of my gear, rifle, helmet and flak jacket and with the pistol in my right hand and a flashlight in the other, I slid into a 3 foot by 3 foot tunnel to see what I could find. It was lined with bamboo along the top and sides and very dark and I kept the .45 pointed directly in front of me, expecting to see the enemy at close range any second. I went in quite a long way, but I didn't find anything or anyone, I am very happy to say. It was my one and only time as a "Tunnel Rat."

After I had been in the field for a couple of months, we went to the "rear" – the infantry 2nd Battalion position. We were going to get showers, a hot meal, and watch a movie – *Alfie* with Michael Caine – so we went to our tent and stripped off all the dirty clothes and after wrapping towels around our bodies, my radio operator R and I put on flip-flops and headed for the showers. But as we passed the battalion radio tent, R heard something and wanted to stop and look into the tent to see what was going on. As we listened, we heard Lt. S calling for artillery support and when we plotted the grid location on a map, we could see that he was either scared or confused or both and he was calling for artillery on his own location. I got on the radio and told him that we'd be right there – we could hear his firefight about two or three kilometers away. The radio operator on duty, a guy who said he had been a Mouseketeer on the Disney program (he had a photo of himself with Mickey Mouse ears and his name on a T-shirt on his field desk) offered to take us as close as we could drive in his jeep and after we raced to our tent, put on pants and boots and our flak jackets, cartridge belts and rifle, we raced in the gathering dark towards the sound of Lt. S's platoon fighting. As we came to the edge of the rice paddies, our Mouseketeer friend went back, and Cpl. R and I headed for the dark tree line between us and S's platoon. It was easy to see what direction to take because of the visible tracers from the firefight above the trees, and a long trail of litter dropped by those Marines – magazines, bayonets, C-Rations, and some grenades, which I picked up as I spotted them. Cpl. R and I had been running but as we approached the large open area on the other side of the tree line, everything went quiet, and it was fully dark now. I called Lt. S on our radio and told him that we were coming in and he asked us if we had a flare and I told him that I did – and I fired a red pencil flare straight up. He saw us and told us to come ahead. When we had joined up with his platoon, grouped in a circle at the center of the open area, I asked him where he wanted the artillery and he told us: "Where you just came out of the tree line." I told him that the enemy was gone when we came through, so we were not really needed anymore.

Lt. S had four casualties which he evacuated using the Mechanical Mules he had with him – I was surprised and a bit angry because he had made the strange decision to bring those noisy damn things with him on that patrol. Worse, the poor casualties were going to get really battered on their way to the rear, carried on those rough-riding, flat and hard vehicles. Well, I wasn't the Lieutenant.

Now Cpl. R and I were stuck with Lt. S's platoon for another several weeks, and all we had was our basic "war" gear and no shirts, underwear or socks. Never did get that shower.

Going Home on Basket Leave

JUST AS I WAS PRETTY WELL ALONG IN MY NEW JOB, I WAS CALLED in to go home on leave: when you extended your tour in Vietnam you were given 30 days of leave wherever you wanted to go. Like a dummy, I picked home. I should have picked Paris, or Tokyo or somewhere else.

We stopped briefly in Okinawa to retrieve our sea bags with our other uniforms and got a lecture from a Staff NCO that we should "put all of our experiences in a wall locker" and not try to share anything with the people at home. He was right, but that didn't stop us from finding out the hard way. I remember arguments among us about "who saw the most combat," with a young infantry Marine angrily and tearfully telling us that we were all "rear area commandos" and hadn't experienced what he had. He was right: the Grunts had their own uniquely dangerous war, and I couldn't blame him for feeling the way he did.

I also remember meeting a young Marine sweeping our barracks who was terribly disfigured: he had long, deep scars visible on his arms and his face – in some places his bone showing through his skin, and you could see his teeth through the skin that covered the left side of his jaw – and he wore thick glasses. He showed me a photo of what he looked like before and he had been a handsome guy. He told me that he had been hit by a white phosphorus booby trap and had been burned and that he had asked the Marine Corps to keep him in Okinawa and to never send him home again.

We were searched fairly thoroughly for contraband (weapons, "meat photos" of the dead enemy, etc.) and I think that most objects got through their inspections. I remember two Marines showing me their M1 Thompson submachineguns in the barracks after their "inspection."

At this point it should probably go without saying that all of this warfare had an effect on us. The effects were there all right and some of those effects were pretty obnoxious. I for one, came home with a pronounced resentment for the civilians back in the "World" (which was what we called the US) and no little bit of psychological disturbance. In hindsight, it would be a lot better to bring people back from that kind of environment in slow stages to kind of let the hostility and fear ease before returning us to "civilized" society. Ah, but they didn't. It also didn't help that the so-called "antiwar" movement was picking up steam and more and more of our fellow Americans were finding better excuses for staying out of combat/helping the enemy along. As I mentioned earlier, we were getting some harassment in Vietnam through pro-enemy leaflets that these groups were printing for the enemy's use, and we had heard that some of our guys were being jeered and spat on when they got off the planes coming home. I got into El Toro Marine Corps Air Station near Santa Ana sometime just before midnight, so there wasn't any kind of reception, good or bad waiting for us when got there. In something less than 96 hours from leaving Vietnam, I was back in LA and heading into the San Fernando Valley in a taxi heading for my parent's house. Well, almost: The taxi driver cheated me and dropped me off about two miles from home and I had to hike the rest of way with my seabag over my shoulder.

My parents weren't up at three or so in the morning when I finally made it to their door, so I found an unlocked back window and crawled through. I found a top bunk that didn't have a brother or sister in it and lay down, still in my full uniform and went to sleep. It is impossible to get into a small house unobserved with a big family – my little sister Julie (age 4 at that time) – alerted everyone to a stranger in the house – but I wasn't aware of that because I was already deeply asleep. When I woke up, my mother and father, sisters and brothers were standing around my bunk, watching me. They were a little put out that I missed their hand-made "Welcome Home" banner inside the front door, but they were excited that I was back.

The weekend that I got back it was Easter 1967. My family being my family, we all went to Mass (I think it was Our Lady of Peace Church, but I'm not sure) and we got there early so everybody could sit down. Catholics are like everybody else: you get the most participation on the big holy days and that's it – and Easter was a big one. My family filled the whole pew with Mom and Dad, my brother Dave and his wife Debbie and his daughter Denise and all the rest of my brothers and sisters – a total of fourteen people, counting me. I sat in my uniform at the end of the pew near the wall. It slowly sank in that not only was I the only one there in uniform, but there were bunches of other young men of military age all over the church. It was a beautiful spring day with the sun shining and that, as far as I could tell, was all that anyone had on their minds. My friends were out there patrolling at the same time, and some were probably dying . . . and so my thoughts went, as I got angrier and angrier sitting in that pew. Just at this time, a large red-faced man who was serving as usher leaned down to where I was sitting and said, "Tell those people to move down!"

I looked up at him and said, "What's the matter, you too f—ing tired to be polite? Those people are my family." He said something angry which I've since forgotten, then I hit him or shoved him, which knocked him down on his back on the floor. My dad hustled me out of Mass and as well as I can remember, I was never asked to go to Mass with my family again.

I went to see high school buddies but that was a dumb thing to do. I resented them being away from the fight and they asked stupid questions like "did you kill anybody?" and "how's it feel to kill somebody?"

At least I had my Honda 305 Scrambler motorcycle (replacing the one my brother wrecked while I was in boot camp), and I took it for long rides away from everyone.

I took a girl I knew from before – Ann – to see a movie, *A Man and a Woman*, at a theater in Westwood near UCLA and of course, went in uniform. My date was a bit uncomfortable, since I was getting stares while we were waiting in line, and they weren't friendly stares. Once we got to our seats near the rear in the theater, the presentation opened with a film showing the American flag and playing the National Anthem. I immediately stood at attention and so did my date. Nobody else stood. So, I yelled: "GET OFF YOUR GOD-DAMN BUTTS!" and everyone suddenly stood (I can be quite loud) and a few looked back towards me, nervously. When the last notes of the Anthem were finished, I said "take your seats!" And they did.

Needless to say, it was a lousy date after that, and Ann never had a thing further to do with me.

I went to a department store in Van Nuys to visit another girlfriend at her job there, and just as I was entering the large sliding glass doors, a car backfired behind me. I hit the floor immediately and the two tall glass doors closed on me, trapping me between them on the floor. While I was struggling there, a sweet older women approached me and asked me what the matter was and I said "epilepsy, Ma'am," got up and left.

My Mom and Dad put together a welcome home party which included two young ladies; L, an old friend of mine and a coworker's daughter, B. B and I dated a few times and despite my wound-spring mental state I remember that we had fun. I had a favorite picture of her, up standing on some branches in a tree, laughing that I carried with me when I went back. I was very happy to get on the plane and get back to my company in Vietnam.

My little brother and I on my Scrambler during my Basket Leave home from Vietnam. (Photo from the Author's Collection)

Returning to Vietnam

ONCE I GOT BACK WITH ECHO COMPANY, WE WERE IMMEDIATELY back into intense activity and I was once again immersed in what was now familiar and comfortable, patrolling. I was happy to see that most of my friends were still there and that we hadn't lost anyone I knew while I was gone. The main thing I saw when I got back was that everyone had the new M-16 rifle instead of our old standby, the M-14. I had my M-14 because it was still where I left it in my tent and for a short while, I coveted the small, light, vicious-looking M-16. But that feeling passed quickly when I saw what was happening with them: they were jamming. Not just jamming but tearing the whole back of the cartridge case off and fusing another fresh cartridge into it, sealing the chamber. The M-16's breech was inaccessible from the outside, so Marines with that kind of jam had to remove the magazine, knock out the sliding pin at the rear of the receiver, pivot the weapon open, remove the bolt and bolt carrier and then use an assembled cleaning rod to knock the jammed case out.

Then you had to reassemble everything, put the magazine back in, chamber a round and attempt to fire again. In an intense firefight, Marines were often killed during that frantic process.

Additionally, the hot new M-16 5.56mm round was not particularly accurate or effective when you hit someone. We had heard all these stories of the new round "tearing off arms and legs" because "it tumbled" but in actual use; it usually made a small hole going in and coming out and men who were hit (you could see the dust coming off their uniforms) just kept running anyway. The sights were difficult to adjust and had no quick way of changing elevation or windage, so we missed a lot more often than before. We complained, but the upper strata of the Pentagon believed that we "weren't cleaning them well enough." The truth was that the ammunition – and the weapon design itself – were defective but that was acknowledged only decades after our war.

Capt. P asked me why I still had the old M-14, when all of the rest of the guys had an M-16. I told him that: "I'm artillery and we don't have the M-16 in the artillery yet" and he said: "Make sure you get one once they have them for you."

And when I went back to the battery for my mail, they'd say "Lindsey, we have an M-16 in the Armory for you."

I'd say: "Naw, the grunts want me to keep my M-14" and I kept that scam going the rest of the time that I was in Vietnam.

I would carry 5-7 loaded magazines, plus a bandoleer of 7.62mm clips. I loaded my magazines from M-60 machine gun belts that I stripped, and I put the tracers (the belts had one tracer per five rounds) into one magazine that I kept in my front left pouch in case a target needed to be pointed out to air support.

People have depicted the guys in Vietnam as sort of bumbling oafs that wandered around from shooting each other to shooting helpless villagers to being clobbered by the VC. The Marines that I saw in the infantry companies were competent, well-led and utterly dangerous to whatever enemy force got near them. No enemy force in its right mind took on a Marine rifle company if they were in equal or even greater numbers. The Marines were aggressive and efficient and unless the enemy were all former track stars for Hanoi U, they were swept up and killed or captured as fast as they could be found and engaged. That, and we weren't stupid. If the enemy had a good piece of ground and appeared to be sticking around, then the grunts would make sure that the doors were closed (platoons slipped around behind the enemy to make sure that they didn't get away) and then somebody like me would get artillery fire and mortar fire and attack jets going on the enemy position, over and over. We're a rich country and we had plenty of artillery ammunition and bombs.

A very prominent feature in the infantry world in Vietnam were the mines and booby traps. Almost every trail, the tops of dikes in the rice paddies, the gates and sometimes even people were loaded with explosives or lethal spikes to kill and maim us. The most common booby trap in our area was the grenade in the can. The VC would nail a can (usually one of our green C-Ration cans) about a foot or so off the ground to a small tree. A grenade (also usually one of ours) was inserted into the can, with the safety lever shortened so it was barely held by the lip of the can. The fuze on the grenade had been shortened to instantaneous and a slack wire, usually very thin and green in color would be attached to the grenade and to another tree or stake on the other side of the trail. The wire was always concealed in the grass, so all it took was a toe lightly hooking the wire to set off the grenade and it would wound or kill several men at once. There were many, many other types: The "Bouncing Betty" which went off when a small wire trigger was deflected or a tripwire was pulled and fired a bomb six feet in the air and then detonated, sending steel ball bearings at head height. We had the "Toe Poppers," small plastic mines that were shallowly buried and tore feet off when stepped on. The enemy hung dud artillery shells in the trees to cause a horribly lethal airburst over us when tripped and they littered the trails with small pits that covered iron sharpened stakes to impale feet when you stepped on them.

This constant danger of walking anywhere produced the effect of causing us to simultaneously be watching ahead and to the flanks for any change of color or odd movement to watch for ambushes while always watching the trail ahead of you for wires, triggers and pits. Only the very attentive and skilled survived – and sometimes even they didn't make it.

You learned that wearing sunglasses was stupid, because you needed to see the small changes in color that gave away an enemy hiding in the brush, or the thread-like tripwires of the booby traps concealed in front of us. Nobody made noise, nobody smoked, no one wore any kind of scent. Nobody who valued life ever smoked dope either – anything that disturbed the clarity of your mind was dangerous. No matter where you were, the margin between us and the enemy winning was who smelled, heard, or sensed the other first. I can remember distinctly smelling the enemy when they were near, either from the smell of their tobacco smoke or for their unique body odor.

The scariest times for us were when we emerged from the cover into the open and faced a dark tree line ahead of us across a wide-open area and of course, nighttime movement. You watched the dark depths of the tree lines in front of you, staring intently for any movement, any sign that the enemy was waiting to open fire. Once you were out in the open, there was no cover, no protection, and those long stretches of walking in the open were deeply frightening. At any split second, the far tree line could and sometimes did, erupt in flashes and clouds of dust and the air crackling around you as the enemy began firing. Your only hope when that happened, was to take them under accurate fire as rapidly as you could and rush at them to get into those dark areas in front of us and kill them before they killed all of us.

I changed. I started out as a young, relatively innocent young man and piece by piece became much different than before. I had seen our own guys die, all around me. It wrenches you to see young guys just like you dead or horribly, irrevocably mutilated. Dead men seem like a pile of rags where before they were just like you, young and alive and hopeful. You can see death take place when the eyes film over and flies start landing on them. It fills you with anger and a rising drive for revenge when your own people die. It also fills you with sadness that this young man died and you somehow you made it.

Conversely, seeing the enemy dead made me happy. The feeling was "got the bastard before he got any more of us." I found that I had gotten hardened, and I had no trouble at all aiming and shooting and doing my best to hit and kill the enemy troops I saw. I'd even shoot them again and again to make sure that were dead. I found that I had an animal center that I hadn't been aware of and even now, long after the war, I can't summon an ounce of regret.

One other thing: combat was addictive. Your senses were primed to their utmost, you could hear even the faintest noises, you could smell the distinctive smells of the enemy, you could see the faint color changes or furtive movements of someone hidden in the brush. It was hunting with the strong chance that the other hunter would get you. Long after the war, normal day-to-day activities were profoundly disappointing because the full self we had discovered in ourselves wasn't exercised anymore.

Not everyone got there. A friend of mine used to say that there are three kinds of people: Killers, Fillers, and Fodder.

"Killers" were the men with the instincts and developed their abilities quickly enough to be vital to a unit. They aimed when others were ducking or hiding, they knew the best approach to take advantage of terrain, they didn't freeze up or get rattled. They were the hard center of any combat unit and usually made up maybe 15-20% of the unit if you were lucky.

"Fillers" were the majority. They were solid and dependable but often didn't aim when they were firing. Just hosed rounds, hoping they'd hit something or more likely, just to get the enemy to stop shooting at them. Sometimes they'd freeze in fear, sometimes they'd do something impulsive and irrational, and sometimes, maybe often, suffer psychological shock from their experiences. We used to call it the "shakes" and the ones with the shakes were called

"Shaky Jakes." It wasn't meant as an insult because everyone understood. Sometimes things were too hard to deal with and the brain crapped out on you. Fillers sometimes became Killers if they lived long enough.

"Fodder" were guys that just weren't suited for combat through their mental makeup and/or lack of instincts. That doesn't mean that everyone who was killed was Fodder, since everyone could be and was killed – it's combat. But Fodder were people who never learned anything: you could train them, coach them, guide them but they were going to screw up fatally. It was only a matter of time. They would stand on the skyline, smoke cigarettes at night on outpost or ambush, didn't watch where they put their feet on trails, opened gates even when you warned them not to, and they were dangerous to anyone around them when they fired their weapons. I think that they didn't amount to more than 5% but that's because the Marine Corps had an excellent winnowing process. The main thing was to get them out of combat if you could but if you couldn't, you had to stay as far from them as you could.

NAVY CORPSMEN

The Marine Corps didn't have a medical branch: the medics we had were called Corpsmen and they were assigned from the navy to us. We made fun of them back in garrison, calling them "Squids" and "Pecker checkers" (from their duty to inspect us for venereal diseases) and strongly implied that they were gay – but when they joined us in combat, nobody was more important or more revered. Squids they were, but whenever or wherever you were hurt, they were right there, oblivious of the extreme danger. They were profoundly brave and nobody who has ever served with them in combat has anything but reverence for the crazy, selfless bravery of our Corpsmen. It would be close to impossible to ever count up how many lives they saved – or how many of them died while trying to save us.

MEDICAL EVACUATION ("MEDEVAC") PILOTS

Our war was the true initiation of using helicopters for almost all of our emergency evacuation of casualties. There was some limited use of helicopters in the Korean War but nothing like the scale we saw in Vietnam. Every day, day after day, in almost all weather and conditions and despite heavy enemy fire, our Marine medevac helicopter pilots got in and got us when we needed them. The courage to do that job defies imagination: helicopters are noisy, low-flying and obvious. The enemy doesn't have to be particularly skilled to hit a helicopter and almost anything they fired would enter one side and go out the other at any point. There was little or no armor on helicopters, so they had all of the bullet resistance of a soda can. If a helicopter's rotors are hit and they fail, there is no escape from the fatal fall that will come. No parachutes and no hope. Many helicopters, mostly the jet-powered ones, burned like a torch when they were hit, and usually burned up almost completely before they got to the ground.

Despite this, our medevac pilots always came for us, always. I remember a Marine UH-34 coming for an emergency medevac on a pitch-dark night. The only visual guide we could give him was three white flashlights, each shrouded from side view by the body of a C-Ration tin can. The Landing Zone (LZ) was so tightly framed by tall trees that we weren't completely sure that we could get him in, but he flew in anyway, rotor tips smacking tree limbs all around him in the total dark. He got our casualties out!

There have never been braver men than medevac pilots.

Combat Operations

THE INFANTRY MOVED A LOT AT NIGHT, AND IT WAS EFFECTIVE BUT always frightening. I don't have particularly great night vision and like I said earlier, I wear glasses for nearsightedness, so sometimes I felt nearly blind. We would sleep for an hour or two and get moving again and I think that most sleep I ever got, day to day was about four hours per 24 hours. Somehow, we got used to that routine and other than feeling a lack of energy during the middle heat of the day, we functioned well. Night movements were how we often found the enemy because they moved at night too. During one patrol, we stopped in a deserted house with the usual thatched sides and dirt floors and we picked it as a good place to halt and catch a little sleep until the rest of the company began to move again. I went inside with a couple of other Marines, and I picked a circular woven winnowing mat for my bed, laid my rifle on its bipod legs pointing out the open door and went to sleep. We had that ability to sleep instantly when we got any opportunity to do so. After some period of time, I snapped awake and saw a man with a rifle standing in the door, the moonlight behind him and it was also instantly obvious that this guy was a VC, and he was just getting home from his night patrol and maybe was just that same second aware that someone was in his house.

I reached for my rifle and immediately shot him with a burst of fire, and he fell straight down in a heap. Then the rest of his squad that had gotten some short distance away, likely after dropping him off, opened fire at us and we scrambled to a nearby riverbank, vaulted over the lip and returned fire. This closely matched fight escalated when the rest of our company joined in, and the VC ran off. I don't know if we got any more of them but none of us were hit.

Which is something characteristic of night gunfights: lots of rounds fired, grenades thrown, mayhem in all directions but usually very few casualties. It's hard to hit people at night unless they are right there in front of you as my VC had been. I've witnessed many night engagements and often there weren't anybody hit on either side even though thousands of rounds were fired. There was even an instance in early 1966 when a Marine rifle company inadvertently approached a Marine artillery battery at night and a gunfight started between those Marines and both sides fired until they were almost out of ammunition and then someone recognized that both units were heavily engaged and calling for help – at the same location. Not a scratch on anyone.

It would rain like nothing else you've ever seen and you'd go for weeks without ever being warm or dry and the fungus would eat at your feet if you didn't figure some way of drying them every once in a while. Spare dry socks were critical. We didn't wear underwear in the field because it chafed and caused sores and it rotted off soon anyway. Pictures from home or other valuable bits of paper would disintegrate or be eaten by more fungus and cameras would rust solid, never to work again. When patrolling, you had to keep down in the deep mud of the rice paddies because everyone knew that the VC mined the dikes. Great choice: hip-deep or deeper in water all the time or climb up on the dikes and blow yourself up. Our bases were on high bits of ground, so we could keep out of the water some of the time, but the snakes and the rats swarmed up to that same piece of ground with you to stay out of the water. Not much fun, since Vietnam's snakes went from poisonous to <u>really</u> poisonous. They had one little green snake called a Bamboo Viper that we called the "Two Step"; one step you're bitten—second step, you're dead. Luckily, that was a relatively rare snake and not very aggressive. It didn't have to be.

Night was the worst. It would get unbelievably dark some nights and the enemy could sneak in very close to you and you wouldn't find out until they were right there in front of you. If you were moving – and we often did our moving at night – your eyes would just get used to the pitch dark when some bozo from somewhere else would drop a big aircraft flare or fire an artillery flare over you. The brilliant light of a magnesium flare hanging from a parachute would silhouette all of us to the full view of the enemy in dazzling, blinding white light and destroy what little night vision we had built up to that point. When that happened, we'd all drop to the ground fast and cover our eyes to try to preserve our night vision and quietly wait until the flare sputtered out and fell to the ground. Then the front of the column would get to their feet and then the middle and then the end until we were all rushing forward to get into the quiet dark of the trees. We would grope through the tree lines carefully, holding on to each other's pack straps to keep from losing connection with each other. When the point man moved forward, he would use a thin stick to feel in front of him from his head height to his feet, one step at a time to see if there were any tripwires in our path. When he found one, he would lean back in the dark and guide the fingers of the man behind him to the wire and whisper "mine" in his ear. Each man following would do the same thing until we were past the tripwire.

The point of all of this movement at night was to catch the enemy by surprise at first light and it often worked. Sometimes we'd run into small pockets of the enemy and there would be a short and vicious firefight and we'd kill or capture some VC. Sometimes we'd run into what we were hoping for, a really large bunch of the enemy and the fight would develop into long periods of heavy firing, punctuated by grenades, mortars, and rockets. Big firefights were hard to describe: the first few shots would suddenly build into an enormous roar as hundreds of scared men on both sides turned loose in each other's directions, firing weapons that fired hundreds of rounds per minute each. It built into a long, shattering, overwhelming roar, interrupted with the short, hard "slam" of grenades going off. When the rounds came near, they made a loud sharp "pop" (there's a shock wave around a bullet and it makes a sharp crack when it goes by or hits someone), so as you lay down flat on the ground; rounds hit all over the place and bits of dirt and twigs showered all over you. Tracers – bullets with a red or green piece of phosphorus in them – would streak around you as they're fired towards you and then would soar upward as soon as they hit something to burn out, up in the sky. Soon, there are calls for corpsmen, to rush to somebody who'd been wounded. The battles always ended with a slowing of the rate of fire and the enemy's and our dead in the fields and the survivors escaping, then the clouds of red or yellow or green smoke from smoke grenades to mark where the helicopters should land to carry away our wounded and dead.

Sometime during an extended patrol on yet another miserably hot day, a sergeant from our column asked the company commander to hold up for a minute and let him dispose of some captured VC cartridge belts and grenades. He had collected them from the dead after our morning firefight and now, after noon, those blood-soaked items were covered in flies and stinking. The CO gave his permission and once again, I was asked to cover the men while they destroyed this gear (I think I was picked for this kind of odd extra duty because, as an artilleryman, I was expendable). We moved about 125 meters from our company and found a shallow pit in the open rice paddy – probably an old shell crater – and the sergeant placed a two pound block of C-4 and time fuse in the hole and then placed the cartridge belts with grenades on top. I said that the way he had it set up, the blast would throw the grenades all over the place but was promptly told to mind my own business. They ignited the fuse, and we ran, yelling "fire in the hole" and just as predicted, the grenades flew high in the air and then started going off all over, like a self-generated mortar attack. This time, luck favored the dimwitted and nobody was hurt.

On one night, our company holed up in yet another deserted village and I got ready to register targets for the evening. Once again Capt. P disagreed with the grid position I had for where we were and for some reason, convinced me that I was off by 1,000 meters. I used his grid reference and fired my first registration round (HC smoke again) at my southernmost target. We heard a loud bang and smoke poured out of a hole almost under where Capt. P had set up his Command Post (CP). I should have stuck to my guns about my map spot (or picked a target farther away). Very impressive when your own rounds hit right next to where you're standing.

A little later that evening, one of the grunts found the opening of a tunnel under us. We surrounded the opening and the Captain called for an illumination grenade to be thrown into the cave. Illumination grenades are shaped just like our M-26 frag grenades but are a little lighter, have a distinct lip on the bottom and have an 11 second fuze. When they go off, they produce a brilliant white magnesium flame and light up everything very clearly.

The Marine threw the illumination grenade and I stood in front of the opening, rifle ready.

My mind wandered just a little and I thought: "what if that wasn't an illum grenade?" so I stepped to the left of the opening.

Then Pow! The frag grenade that was supposed to be an illum grenade went off, knocking me over, stunned, to the ground.

Later, when it started to get light, some Marines started pointing at me and laughing. It turned out that the "cave" was a cooking pit of some sort and the grenade had blasted fine black soot over every inch of me and I was solidly black from head to toe.

In April 1967, I was transferred to Golf Company, and we were on an operation south and west of Danang and it was the beginning phase of a regiment-sized attack on a suspected Vietcong battalion headquarters. The plan as briefed, was that we would infiltrate by platoons by night after staging from a CAP unit (Combined Action Program – a Marine squad that lived with and protected a set of villages). Then after moving most of the night, join up with the rest of our company that next day, then our company would link up with the rest of the battalion and we would assault near dawn the day after.

The whole thing required what I considered the most nerve-wracking kind of movement in Vietnam: slow, steady walking in long lines being as silent as possible through enemy-held territory. We kicked off from the CAP just after midnight and moved down narrow trails threading through dark canyons of dense woods and thickets and extreme dark. The trails started with an archway above us, woven from vines with a star at the center, more or less announcing that you had entered the enemy's home turf.

The trails were also mined, so each step was taken slowly and deliberately, and the tension was immense.

After several hours of this, we found an open area by the tree line and settled in for a couple of hours' sleep. When I woke, I rolled to one side and noticed some odd coloration beside me. Next to where I had been sleeping, there was a large section of wicker, covered with dirt and leaves. It was the covering for a Tiger Pit, a deep (6 feet) rectangular hole with sharpened iron stakes at the bottom and I had been sleeping right next to it for the last couple of hours. I tell my family that "my Guardian Angel is a big, muscular guy with tattoos and scars": he was working overtime that night.

It was just daylight and the word went around that two Marines were missing. We scanned all around to see if we could see them and as we were looking, we heard two shots across that open area and then two Marines in the distance emerged from cover, dragging two dead VC behind them. They had gotten separated from us during the night and had stopped to wait for daylight and had started to eat a C-Ration breakfast when two VC ran directly into them, and their makeshift campsite and they shot them both. We resumed our march and met up with the rest of the company and headed for the next point.

During our movement, we could tell that the enemy was watching us, moving parallel to us in the tree lines about 400m meters away.

It was that evening when the VC infiltrator killed our two Marines on outpost on our company perimeter and later that very dark night when our Dog Handler shot and killed that infiltrator I mentioned at the beginning of this book.

A helicopter came in to take away our two dead from that night and we got some sort of news reporter and his Japanese cameraman along with our new ammunition and C-Rations. He wore a bush jacket and had longish blond curly hair and he made it clear as soon as he landed that he thought that we were all war criminals and focused most of his time taking footage of the dead VC in our midst and audibly criticizing us.

We were a hard bunch and he realized fairly quickly that we weren't going to put up with too much from him – so he and his camera man left quickly and took the next helicopter out again.

We had an older man accompanying us too who said he was a writer. He seemed like a really nice guy, but I never got his name or found out what he wrote. It seemed odd to allow a guy of his age to be out with us, unarmed and exposed to the same dangers as we were.

When the helicopters came in to supply us, they carried the very much anticipated bags of mail and sometimes the "Sundries Pack": a large box that was provided to units of a hundred men when they were in the field for a while. It contained cigarettes, tropical chocolate, chewing tobacco, shaving supplies, soap, chewing gum and I think toilet paper, but most important to me, cigars – Roi Tan Panatelas, to be exact. I knew exactly where they'd be located in the box, so I'd race out to it, slice the box at the correct point and remove the cigar box. I had developed the completely silly and superstitious belief that if I had a cigar in my mouth, nothing would happen to me. The infantry Company Gunny would come out to get the cigars from the box, but it was too late: I already had them tucked into my flak vest. A bit later, I'd give him one "I'd found" if he looked too disappointed.

We began the approach march to our objective, linking up with the rest of our battalion, and the day got hotter. We were moving through a succession of open areas and tree lines and as always, we approached every potential cover for the enemy with wariness. Foxtrot Company ahead of us, hit a large booby trap and it was a monster. After you had spent some time in Vietnam, your ear became tuned to explosions, and you could tell by the sound what kind of thing went off and you could pick out the screams mixed in with the detonation. This one was a 155m howitzer round suspended in the trees and it killed more than a dozen Marines and wounded several more. I won't describe what I saw.

Sometime mid-morning, the other two battalions were in their blocking positions on the other sides of the objective, a long thin tree line on the edge of a long, open field of tall yellow grass. I was in the center of our company which was in reserve, right behind the two assaulting companies – so I just broke into the open when the lead companies ran into the enemy defenses. The enemy opened up with several machineguns, including one heavy machine gun and we took casualties immediately. The leading companies recoiled and returned fire and the volume of fire, the noise was deafening. I had never heard that much sustained fire in my life, and it was obvious that it really was an enemy battalion, and they were staying put.

I lay down flat in the grass and tried to send an artillery fire mission, but the medevacs were already going, and a Sav-A-Plane was in effect that stopped all artillery and mortar fire in our area until the evacuations were done. I remember hearing the bullets crack as they went by and seeing long lines of grass fall where the bullets cut through. We were pinned down and it looked like it was going to be really tough to cross that 300-400m of open ground to get to them when it was our turn to attack.

While I was lying there, a single Marine F-4 Phantom approached and crossed over me, very low and perpendicular to the enemy line. Our Forward Air Controller (FAC) must've had him under his control because the F-4 made his pass and then turned around us one more time and passed directly over me again to make his bombing run. We were one edge of a small triangle bordered by three Marine battalions, separated by only a few hundred meters, so he had to drop whatever he had with extraordinary precision or he would kill some of us. So, he was flying very low and slow – so slow that the plane was making that distinctive moaning sound Phantoms usually made when they were slowing for landing. Then I saw a whole, solid wall of muzzle flashes coming from the enemy tree line and the enemy was standing up, at least a hundred of them, pouring fire at that Phantom as he approached. Without flinching, that pilot dropped four "Snakeye" 500 pound bombs (The Snakeye had a tail fin assembly that popped open upon release to form a broad cross at the rear of the bomb, slowing it drastically to allow the bombing aircraft to escape the blast.).

They fell directly on the enemy position and huge clouds of dirt, debris, rooftops and trees soared high in the air and after the stunning concussions of the blasts faded, all the enemy fire stopped, and we raced up and forward to get them. When we got into their position, we discovered that the enemy had concrete and sandbag bunkers, barbed wire and mines but the four bombs killed many of them and those that could run away, ran into our blocking battalions and we could hear the gunfire in their direction.

I saw that Phantom turning towards Danang. There was smoke behind him but with Phantoms always smoking it was hard to tell if he had been badly hit or not. I would love to find out who the pilot was and buy him a case of whatever he wanted to drink.

I think that at some point, maybe months before, I realized that death wasn't that frightening anymore. You developed a sort of resignation that the law of averages was going to catch up with you and you'd be killed. I used to search the enemy dead looking for ID or a wallet or something of interest, so I filled my own wallet with pretty girls' photos and a photo of a BSA Lightning motorcycle and a picture of a 289 Cobra sports car and the only purpose of that wallet was to give whichever enemy soldier who killed me the best possible souvenir – that he'd think that he had killed the "biggest stud in the 1st Marine Division." That was the frame of mind we developed, and it still seems funny to me. When you're dead, you're dead.

I had also picked up the habit of shooting whoever I hit after they went down, usually a burst of three rounds, just to make sure he stayed down. Writing about it now, it seems strange, but we had hardened and killing had become almost comfortable. One less enemy left. I wish I could say that I regret it now, but I don't. Some years later, I was hunting ducks from a blind on the Dam Neck naval base with a German naval officer friend when I hit two ducks as they were coming in to land. One of the ducks had apparently only been lightly hit and was swimming away. I stood up and shot the wounded duck twice more and my German friend was understandably horrified. I didn't know what to say, other than "it's a habit."

Operations south and west of Hill 55, around Phoung Luc – where the big assault took place – continued further as we pursued more of the enemy main force elements. We moved in long, snaking lines across small rivers and through deserted villages and we were in large enough numbers that the enemy continued to avoid us rather than engage. I remember that we overran an enemy R&R facility in a large white building that had a swimming pool and we captured some of their prostitutes, wearing a lot of makeup and the first miniskirts we had ever seen. They were terrified of us, but we were gentle with them and passed them back to the headquarters element for evacuation. I also remember finding small green bananas growing in a grove and taking a small bunch of them and sticking them under my right suspender strap so we could eat them later. We came up to a single thick pole bridge with a single rope for hand support across a narrow but rough river and while I was crossing – one hand on the rope, one hand on my rifle – our battalion commander, LtCol H, yelled: "hey you, 'bananas for epaulettes' – use both hands!" and I grinned back at him and complied. A little later, the colonel H called me up to where he was sitting with his staff and angrily warned me about my wearing a small round VC hat (which had an American Flag patch sewn to the side) instead of my helmet. He said that if saw me wearing it again, "he'd give it to his mortarmen to blow it off the tube when they fired it." I put my helmet on and stuffed that hat into my suspender straps – then as soon as I was around the corner, put the hat back on to laughter from the officers. The Colonel was a fine man and always communicated competence and affection.

While I'm describing our colonel, I need to mention the quality of the 2nd battalion's young officers and Staff NCOs; unlike the officers and Staff NCOs I spoke about in the artillery battery, the infantry lieutenants and the artillery Forward Observers – also lieutenants – were younger, closer to our age, and closer to us. We trusted them and they trusted us. If someone (like me) raised his hand to halt the column and get the lieutenant or Staff sergeant's attention, they would come to us and ask us what we knew and often took our advice. I did that one time near the An Trach church. I felt that chill that told me things were wrong, raised my hand and the lieutenant asked me what it was. I told him that I was sure that someone was ahead of us and to our left. He asked me what I recommended, and I suggested pushing off the trail 90 degrees to our left and then coming up behind the area 50 meters to our front. We did that and surprised several VC and after a short, brisk firefight, chased them off.

The Infantry Staff NCOs were only slightly older than us but experienced and competent. We listened to them and their advice carefully because they knew what they were talking about, and our survival depended on them.

During our next operation, our Forward Air Controller called for air support while we were with him and the F-4s we got absolutely obliterated the wrong tree line, about a kilometer away from where we wanted them. Sometimes, they flew higher and missed even worse. Our preferred Close Air Support were the Marine A-4 "Scooters" and they always flew lower than anything else and had a sterling reputation for courage and precision. I remember one pilot, who was hitting a very dangerous target directly in front of us and he flew from our right to our left very low and dropped napalm exactly on the enemy. He was so low that he flew through his own fireball and when he came out of it, he was trailing flame in the vortices behind his wings and the tail. He did a fast-climbing snap roll and put the flames out. We cheered like we were at an airshow, cheering and yelling "Get some!"

I went back to Bravo Battery every once in a while, to see if I had any mail and to talk to my friends. Most of them had gone home already, so I knew fewer guys there. I had decided that I would extend for another six months again soon, and I would ask to be assigned to a Combined Action Platoon to work with villagers and help them defend themselves. I was committed to our war and I planned to stay there as long as it took. I didn't have any illusions about my chances though. While I was back at Bravo, the battery gunny put me on Tower Watch (the Staff NCO mentality at Bravo hadn't changed any) and while I was in the tower, I heard footsteps on the ladder. I looked down and it was a lieutenant climbing up to see me. He said: "my name is lieutenant P__G__ III, – but you can call me '"Sir"' – I laughed, and he showed me his graduation photo from the Naval Academy with him in his dress whites and his sword. He was my new Forward Observer and team leader and he had heard that I was experienced, and he wanted to talk.

He and I went to Golf Company and we went out on local sweeps around An Trach, following the river that ran north and south. We didn't run into anything big for a while, so he stayed with the company commander while I went out with the platoon patrols. The platoon I was with found a white-painted wooden Vietcong barracks building well hidden in some trees and the area was deserted. There was a sugar cane press that was powered by two water buffalos and a vat of molasses next to the barracks and if we had any doubt about who the owners were, there was a portrait of Ho Chi Minh on the wall inside. I found a panji pit near the entrance and when I lifted the edge of the mat covering it, I saw a Bamboo Viper that was kept in that pit with a short length of fishing line tied to its tail. We killed the snake and then booby trapped the building with blocks of C-4 under the front steps.

We left and headed back to the company CP and heard an explosion behind us when somebody hit those front steps. We were engaged by the enemy immediately from the direction of the barracks after this and the firefight lasted about ten minutes. There were two villagers, two women harvesting peanuts, caught in the middle of the firefight and they stayed flat on the ground and weren't hit. Nobody among us was hit, either.

When we got back to the CP, it was midday and as always, crazy hard-to-breathe hot; so we stayed where we were. Lt. G asked me to look for a well to replenish our water and naturally when I said I'd go, everybody around asked me to fill their canteens too. I took my flak jacket and helmet off and left my M-14 behind and had maybe ten empty canteens in my arms and as I headed across a small trail, I caught sight of someone in white to my left, maybe 30 yards away. The man, completely dressed in white, fired at me several times as I dove for the brush in front of me, scattering the canteens I had bundled in my arms.

The grunts in the CP ran and caught that VC and took his weapon away. He was maybe 17 years old and scared and when he sat down, he started to sit on my rifle (which was propped up on its bipod – (note the photo of a rifle like mine in Appendix I)) until he saw that suddenly, everyone around him was pointing rifles at him and he realized with terror what he was sitting on, and he moved to a stump to sit. He had an old rusty M-1 rifle and as we found out later that he had only been issued that thing a week before when he was taken from his parent's home and told to "go kill Americans." I gave him a cigarette and he motioned me closer and then lifted his shirt – he had a VC stick grenade in his waistband, and he wanted me to take it from him.

Other than scaring everybody, he hadn't hurt anyone – so our company commander elected to take our teenage prisoner to his parents' house and hand him off to them, making them promise to hide him from the VC. We kept the rifle and the grenade.

We patrolled farther down the river later and we still needed to fill canteens. I was elected – again – to fill the damn things, so I waded to the middle of this small river where the water looked cleanest, once again with an armload of empty canteens.

One of the greatest fears we had was being caught out in the open in water. You can't move fast in any direction in waist-deep water, and you can see the shots hitting the water around you, so I very cautiously walked out to the middle of the river and started filling canteens.

Then there was an explosion of automatic fire and water kicking up in front of me – I dropped the canteens and struggled to get to the bank and away from the water.

And everybody was laughing, and Lt. G's face was red, and he said," Gee, Rick – you sure have a light trigger!" He had accidentally fired my own full auto M-14 into the water in front of me, when he picked it up to look at it.

Our company was on a local night sweep a little north of Hill 55, following the edge of the Song Yen River that bounded ours and the 7th Marines' Tactical Area of Responsibilities (TAOR). We headed slowly south, searching for the enemy, as always. At first light, I heard a sudden burst of gunfire and saw several Marines firing at a VC that was running away in the open and getting away pretty quickly. Everyone but me was armed with the M-16 and even though several hundred rounds were fired in those few seconds, that guy kept running. I aimed carefully with my M-14 and shot him. We ran up to get him and found that I had hit him in his right hand, chopping off the edge of his hand, taking his little finger with it. He was an older VC – 40 or so – and I could see he was in a lot of pain, so I bandaged his hand with one of my own bandages and gave him a cigarette. He calmed down, since you don't bother bandaging somebody or giving him a cigarette if you're just going to kill him. We found out through our *Chieu Hoi* scout that he was an outpost for an enemy company just ahead of us, so we deployed to meet them—one platoon working around behind the enemy to block them and two platoons to begin the approach to where we thought they were.

APR · 67

Golf Company crossing a VC bridge. The Marine at the start of the bridge is carrying a dead Marine's flak jacket. There was mine on the other side of the bridge and it will go off, moments after this picture was taken. (Photo from the Author's Collection)

APR • 67

A stop for a breather with Golf Company. Note the dried rice paddy. (Photo from the Author's Collection)

We caught up with them near Xuan Diem village at the edge of a large open and dry rice paddy that had been recently plowed. We passed through one tree line and we were starting to cross the wide-open area of that plowed-up paddy, the enemy opened fire. We were experienced, so we were all flat on the ground and we were initially unscathed. We started firing 60mm mortars and some LAW rockets and the enemy, unusually for them, stood their ground and started firing rockets back at us. I detected two machine guns straight across from us, between 150 and 200m away. I started working up an artillery fire mission to hit those positions with 105mm fire. As I waited for the mission to be cleared and to start sending rounds, I saw dust coming up from the window of a house directly across from me – someone was firing from that window. I fired a raking burst just under the window, from right to left and the house began to smolder and burn. I saw a man trying to leave the burning house and I cut him down. Then another one came out of the doorway, and I shot him. By my count, a total of five were lying in a pile outside that door when I was done and the whole house was fully enveloped in fire.

The River of Wounded

MY ARTILLERY FIRE MISSION WAS CANCELLED BECAUSE WE STARTED to get some wounded and a "Sav-A-Plane" was put into effect – so artillery and mortar missions were stopped to allow medevac helicopters to come in without being hit by our own stuff. The platoon to my left started assaulting across the open rice paddy towards the enemy but several of them were hit all at once, five that I could see. I could also see that the enemy was still shooting at the wounded men by the dust kicking up around them. I was only about 50-60m away and in pretty good cover, so with very great reluctance I realized that I was the closest guy to them, and I'd have to go out there and try get them to safety. During those seconds while I was spooling up my nerve, my first-day-in-combat Lt G plopped down next to me and said: "I'll cover you," holding a single-shot M79 40mm grenade launcher. I could see that his safety was on, so I said, "the safety comes off by pushing it forward, Sir" and then I got up and ran for the first guy I could reach.

I left my rifle behind because I'd need both hands and it wouldn't have done me any good to carry a rifle anyway. That plowed paddy was rough and difficult to run on because it was so jumbled up, crooked, and hard. My ankles twisted and I stumbled steadily ahead towards the nearest guy I could reach. I was sure that I was as good as dead, that the next shot would hit me between the eyes. Everybody was shooting and bullets cracked all around me. The Marine I reached had been shot sideways through the hips and his guts were protruding. He was struggling and thrashing around with pain, and I tried to carry him, but he was too tall and too broken to move that way. I tried lifting him and pulling him by lifting under his arms but that didn't work either. His hips were broken, and it hurt him too much. A Marine ran towards us from our tree line, a guy we called "Big John" (I never found out his real name – he was known as our "duty hero" and he had been wounded at least twice before), and he grabbed the wounded guy's feet while I lifted him under his armpits and then we ran towards cover with him between us. Before we got very far, Big John ran out of breath and couldn't go any further; so I had us all lay flat, as low as we could get, and I told Big John to take deep breaths. After a few seconds, we got up again and ran some more, finally reaching the inside edge of our tree line. The wounded Marine – LCpl Dave – was turning blue and I was afraid that he was going to die, so I leaned over him and told him that he "was on the way home." I knew that there were more wounded men out there and I couldn't stall anymore, so I started to stand again to get moving back out into that field when I heard a loud bang and fell immediately next to Dave.

The bullet hit me on the inside left of my right thigh and blew through the outside right of my leg and I just collapsed. I said something like—"Unhh, I'm hit"—and felt intense, stunning pain. It felt like someone had taken a sledgehammer to my leg and crushed it, which was a fairly accurate analysis. There was no feeling of impact at all when the bullet hit me. My femur was shattered into bits and I was bleeding a lot and the open hole in my greatly expanded leg was too large to cover with my bandages. I grabbed an empty cloth bandoleer and tied it around my upper right thigh next to my crotch and used my Kabar knife to tighten it down to close off the artery and the bleeding. By this time, I felt my blood pool up to my neck while I lay there. A corpsman reached me and tried to get bandages on me, but the holes were just too wide, bigger than my spread-out hand. Big John had also been hit (possibly the same bullet that hit me), so the three of us just lay there, waiting until we got help. I remember feeling guilty that I couldn't just get up and continue helping to get the wounded but there wasn't any way I was going to be able do it. I also remember being very surprised that I had been hit, even though I had seen people hit all around me for months and I had just finished being near-missed by hundreds of rounds. It's funny how our young minds work.

Lt. G crawled up next to me and said, "I'm really sorry you're hurt Rick, but can I have your rifle?" I told him that it was "all his." I called in my own Medevac ("Button Vermillion") – and while I was on the radio, one of the guys from my artillery battery asked which one of us was wounded and using radio jargon I said, "Chinstrap Bravo 61 Alpha, Actual" which meant "me." The voice on the radio said that he was sorry that I was hurt and wished me well. I was told later, that when my battery heard that I was hit, a bunch of them ran to my cot in the gun 5 tent and grabbed all of my souvenirs! Red-headed Lt J, one of the platoon commanders, came by and treated us to a show of bravado to entertain us by firing offhand with his .45 at the enemy while bullets crackled all around him. I said: "Sir, get down, please, you're drawing fire." I was fading from loss of blood, so I don't remember when Dave and Big John were carried to the medevac helicopter, but I remember watching that big Sikorsky UH-34 land in that open paddy while everyone was still shooting. I remember really wanting to be on that plane when I felt a tug on my shoulder, and it was my VC prisoner from that morning. He pointed at the helicopter, and I nodded, and he helped pull me up and he helped carry me to the open door of that bird. I remember watching him waving at me with his bandaged hand as the plane lifted us up and on to Charlie Med in Danang.

When I got to Charlie Med, I was completely naked – they cut your clothes off in preparation for triage – but I still had a frag grenade in my hand in case the helicopter went down. Nobody wanted to be taken prisoner in that neck of the woods, since the local VC were known to torture anyone they captured. There were about a dozen wounded arriving at the same time we did, so there were a lot of men on stretchers lined up on the ground outside the field hospital, waiting to be treated. The corpsmen saw the grenade I had and freaked out, which I thought was funny because grenades are just paperweights until you pull the pin. We had a lot of very badly wounded men there and I remember one who had been horrifically burned by a white phosphorus booby trap and was soaked in blood, from head to toe. The other thing I noticed was how quiet we all were; we were all in almost unimaginable pain but none of us made any noises at all. I was very surprised when they moved me in for treatment first because I thought many were worse off than I was. I was brought into a room, up onto a table and I was bent forward at the waist and a corpsman stuck a long needle into my lower back and then moved in front of me and apologized because his first attempt at a spinal missed. I told him that it's fine, go ahead a try again. He tried again and then there was the most blessed relief you can imagine when that pain finally stopped.

I was put into something they called the "spider," a frame to hold me and my limbs in position and a short curtain was put up at my waist between me and the work they were doing on my leg. From my angle, I was looking up at a large circular reflector around a lamp above us and I could see some of what the surgeons were doing with my leg. The lead surgeon looked at me and said, "we may have to take your leg off – are you OK with this?" I told him to "do what he had to do." He asked me to try to wiggle my toes, which I did, I think – since I couldn't really see what was happening. I talked to the anesthetist while they were working and I said that I looked like an el Greco painting, with all the color of yellow and green in my skin as shown by that reflector. The surgeon turned to him and said, "shut him up!" so he stuck some morphine in my I.V. and I was out.

That following morning, I woke up in a Spica cast, a plaster sheath that enclosed my whole body from the top of my chest down to both feet, with a spreader bar between my legs to keep them about 20 degrees apart, and a 1/8ths inch steel pin drilled through about 3 inches below my right knee. I had tubes all over the place, with freezing cold blood coming through an I.V. in my left arm and I could feel chill blains all the way to my heart. My First Sergeant visited me to see how I was doing and to see if I could still make it back to combat duty, but I think even he was convinced that I wasn't going to be much use for a while and that I should head home.

Happily, there was one area open in that large plaster prison that allowed me to at least an opening to relieve myself at the appropriate times. I was cluttered with tubes to drain me and IVs to fill me and life varied from overwhelming, mind-cramping pain to the blissful float of morphine and sleep.

As mentioned before, my leg was essentially powdered: it's called a "comminuted fracture" and X-rays of my leg looked like a cloud of bone fragments where the largest bone in my body used to be. Nonetheless, I was a happy young man: I was still alive, I still had both of my legs, and I was pleased with myself that little old cowardly me had done something brave for a change. I had come a long way from the days when I avoided the high school thugs who wanted to fight me after school.

Within one or two days, I was packed into an ambulance-configured C-130 to fly to the hospital at Clark Air Force Base in the Philippines. I was so "out of it" that I don't remember any part of that flight. I spent about a week at Clark AFB Hospital, not totally there but I do remember getting all upset and yelling when I discovered Vietnamese wounded right next to me. I had assumed that they were the enemy, and I was furious that they would put me right by them. A military nurse fiercely chewed me out for my attitude and that was the very first encounter of many that I would have with military nurses during my travels to recovery.

I ran into two varieties of military nurse: Navy and Air Force. The Navy nurses would point at their nurse hats with their rank stripes on them and tell us that they were officers, and we would refer to them as "Ma'am." A non-subtle signal that we were at the absolute bottom of the status barrel and should entertain no fantasies of warmth or feminine companionship, God forbid. It's not like we were in any shape to contemplate romance, but a little bit of sweetness would not have encouraged any untoward activities, however long we had been in the bush. Air Force nurses had absolutely nothing but the barest contact with us enlisted swine, leaving any contact with us to others. Both sets of nurses were very warm and friendly with the officer wounded, from what I have heard but they made it very clear to us that we enlisted sorts were beneath contempt. If someone up and melts that "Three nurses" statue at the Vietnam Veteran's Memorial into a puddle of bronze, suspect me. Thermite would work.

I remember that it rained very hard every day while I was at Clark, exactly at 4:00 PM every day. After about a week at Clark, I was loaded onto a bus with racks on either side for stretchers to go on to a plane to go to further critical care in Japan. The one thing I remember while riding in that bus was that we had one guy on a stretcher above me who said that he was a "Seal." I had no idea at that time what that meant – he only struck me as some sort of pale, well-fed sailor who whimpered a lot.

We flew in another C-130 and this time I was only too aware of the flight. It was a long, slow flight to Japan and our stretchers were packed tightly, one above another and I was in a bottom position. The NATO-standard stretcher above me was so close to me that the steel "foot" bar of that stretcher was only a half inch or so from the bridge of my nose. It was claustrophobic, drafty, noisy, and cold for what I remember to be a 12-hour flight. Sometimes I would sneeze, and I would hit the bridge of my nose on that flat piece of steel of the upper stretcher and that would add to the stack of hurt I had in that little box of the bottom rack. I sneezed a lot because it was cold and drafty in that stupid plane. I couldn't see anything except the bottom of that stretcher above me. I couldn't hear anything above the scream of the engines, and unless someone got on their hands and knees, they couldn't see me either. It was like being in a coffin on the floor with just the far-right side open for viewing. The Air

Force nurses stayed at the front of the cabin, and I could just see ankles, fat ankles. To get their attention, for a pain med or to get a piss pot to pee in, I would wave my right arm frantically up and down from my place near the floor. Most of the time, they didn't see me or maybe just ignored me. When one nurse did come to me, she didn't bother lowering herself down to where I was – she would just stick a syringe of Demerol into my I.V. and go back to her conversations up front. That helped with the pain but since I was asking for the piss pot, the situation got more and more frantic for me.

I would wave my arm and the same thick pair of ankles would walk up to my position and stick more Demerol in my I.V., again and again. It was 12-hour flight and I was lucky that I didn't pee in my cast, but it was a very close thing.

I cursed the designer of the stretcher racks for the C-130 aircraft and Air Force nurses will not be beneficiaries in my Will.

We were taken for further intensive care at the Tachikawa Air Force Base hospital near Tokyo and I was put into a small ward with about eight others in the room. Most of the men there were soldiers and most of those were draftees – the first I'd ever met. They had interesting stories with odd differences in culture between the service perspectives of that war. One of the draftee wounded had been shot in the stomach and was in a lot of pain. I asked him how he had been wounded and he told me that a little prettily dressed Vietnamese girl that was about 6 years old and carrying a basket walked by their squad while they were on patrol. He told me that she pulled a .45 from that basket when she was next to him and pointed it at him and shot him. He said that she seemed surprised to see what happened and started to cry. I asked him what happened to her, and he said, "we shot her." I remember being horrified by that – we Marines wouldn't have responded that way, at least I hope not.

The guy in the bed next to me spoke to me in a quiet voice and said that he was a Marine too. He was very weak and depressed, and I asked him what happened to him (I couldn't see him very well because the cast kept me from turning left and down to look at him). He said his name but I don't remember it, but it sounded French-Canadian. He told me that he was on radio watch in the field and that he had fallen asleep when he was supposed to be the one awake. He woke up suddenly with a man standing on his arms, straddling his chest and smiling at him. The VC killed the Marine next to him and then shot the Marine I was speaking to, over and over with an M-1 Carbine, one limb at a time until both arms and both legs were severed. He cried when he told me his story because the guy who was killed next to him was his best friend and was supposed to be asleep, not him. He died very soon after – within one or two days after he told me that story.

The Air Force nurses had very little to do with us. We could hear them talking next door – about the different doctors they were dating – but even if we buzzed for them, they didn't come. All we had were occasional visits by a doctor or two and an injured soldier who was ambulatory who would help us out. This particular soldier was skinny and odd and walked with a stiff gait and had a bandage on the back of his head. I assumed that he was one of the rear-area pogues in Japan who got hurt on liberty or something, so I was a bit pompous with him. He was friendly and cheerful despite my slightly superior attitude and readily emptied and cleaned the bedpans or changed out IVs or got us pain meds or changed the channels on our one TV (all Japanese channels: including *Gunsmoke* dubbed in Japanese and a war movie in which the Japanese sunk one American carrier after another. It was more than a little annoying.). He would cheerfully smuggle Cokes to us and was the one person we could call on, what with the nurses staging some sort of boycott.

I finally deigned to ask him how he got hurt – you know to be nice to him from my lofty "combat veteran" perch – and he told me that he had been hit by a mortar round as it fell nearly straight down, fracturing the back of his skull and then the round hit at his feet, detonating and shearing both feet completely off. I strained over the edge of my bed to look down at his feet and saw that he was walking on rubber pads where his feet had been. God love him, I wish I'd kept his name.

After a week or so at Tachikawa, apparently it was determined that I was fit to move to Yokosuka Naval Hospital. I was stacked into a stretcher-carrying Huey helicopter and flown to a landing pad which featured the complete superstructure of a Japanese WWII cruiser next to it. A pair of soldiers carried my stretcher from there to a bus to take me the rest of the way to the hospital. The soldier at the head end of my stretcher had a gaudy 1st Air Cav patch on his shoulder and while I was looking at that patch, he stumbled and dropped his end of the stretcher. That ripped both I.V.s out of my arms and I yelped with pain, and he said, "Take it on the chin, Buddy." I don't remember what I said back but I doubt if it was Christian.

In Yokosuka we had longer wards and more attentive nurses (it was easy to be more attentive than the Air Force nurses – all you had to do was walk into the room) and Corpsmen. There were also a whole lot more of us on the wards.

We didn't talk much, and I remember at least one Marine died during the two weeks I spent there. I remember that it was sunny in that ward and that the elevators were tiny – for Japanese bodies, I guess – and they had to turn my stretcher diagonally in the elevator and collapse it in width to fit inside.

From there, I was taken in a large and far more comfortable C-141 fitted out with stretchers and flown to Travis Air Force Base between San Francisco and Sacramento California. It was a long, noisy flight but at least I could see out and I had a blanket this time, so I didn't freeze. After a short stop, (just long enough to say "I've been to Travis Air Force Base") I flew in a smaller plane to Camp Pendleton Naval Hospital in Southern California. The funniest story I remember about Travis concerns my Radio Operator, Cpl. R. Five days after I was wounded, R was walking behind a new guy who opened a gate. Before he could shout "Don't open that gate!" the earth suddenly burst upward and R was thrown into the river, blind, deaf and with one broken leg and one broken arm. He floundered around in the water, drowning, when someone reached into the river and got him. After his initial treatment through the usual nodes along the way, he arrived at Travis AFB on a stretcher and one of his eyes slowly opened a bit and he could see through it. The thing he saw first was a young lady in a miniskirt. With his one good arm, he frantically worked to open his other eye and thanks to the young lady with the very short skirt, he could see again!

My experiences so far were like thousands upon thousands of other Marines, soldiers, sailors, and airmen during the Vietnam War. It was an amazingly designed machine that took us out of Vietnam and then funneled us out through many different nodes of treatment and routes the 10,000 miles home. The government did its best to make sure that long-term treatment took place as close to your Home of Record as possible. The fact that there were a quarter million wounded throughout our war, it's nothing less than miraculous that they did so well with this system. I suspect that both our allies and our enemies were astounded that we could pull it off. The only shameful part was that it was done completely out of the public view. We were smuggled in, in groups, anonymously, furtively as though they were ashamed of showing us to anyone.

Camp Pendleton Naval Hospital in those days was a collection of single-floor wooden temporary buildings that had been built to handle WWII casualties and because the Marine Corps never threw anything out, it was still there for us. The exterior was painted a sort of pale grey-green and the interior was a beige (or maybe just really old white) and it was unheated and uncooled and well, temporary. The hospital was in a remote part of Camp Pendleton which is in itself, in a remote part of California, so visitors required a lot of time and dedication to reach us.

When I arrived, the first order of business was to remove the cast. I was strongly in favor of that because it really stank at this point. Imagine, if you will, what a pound of hamburger left outside in the sun for a month would smell like. They "bivalved" (split) the cast into a front half and a back half and then whaled away. I believe that I let out a howl that could be heard all the way to the Main Gate of Pendleton and all I got for that was a stern glare from my doctor, Dr. K, who clearly felt that violently splitting off a big cast over a mashed leg should have been borne with silent grace. Some big Corpsman cut that transverse pin through my leg with a huge pair of bolt cutters (another indecorous howl from me) and then I was installed into a traction rig that hoisted my injured right leg up about 45 degrees and pulled on it, using a system of pulleys, ropes, and weights. That traction rig was to be my home for the next five months.

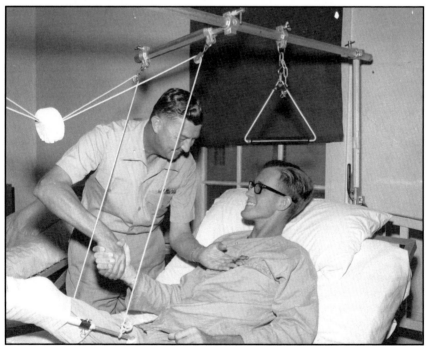

The author in his traction rig. (Photo from the Author's Collection)

I still hurt a lot and the transition from cast to traction had set me back a bit in my progress, pain-wise. I remember that it hurt so bad at first that I could feel people walking in the next ward over and I could tell if it was a man or a woman walking. I was put into a long open ward with about 30 total – 15 on each side – in the room, all osteopathic cases. We had guys blown up by mines, victims of vehicle crashes, and many "missile" wounds (bullets and fragments). When I first got there, I noticed that no one was talking and there was a lot of moaning and calling for more pain meds. The worst offender was a Staff Sergeant directly across from me who had really gotten blown up by a mine. There was no question that he was really badly hurt, but all of his sobbing and cursing was getting everyone else down.

So, I told him to knock it off – "everyone else here is hurt; pipe down." That really set him off and he swore that he'd see me court-martialed. Yeah, OK – but in the meantime, quiet down, you're embarrassing us. Our back and forth "when I get out of here, I'll kick you're a__" and so on kept things interesting and the whining dropped off while they watched me and the Staff Sergeant trade barbs.

Eventually, the Staff Sergeant was shipped on to a hospital in Texas and we all got to know each other. I came up with the idea that we needed more diversion – so if somebody liked Fords, I'd come out for Chevys. If somebody was a Catholic, I'd take the Protestant side and that sort of banter back and forth grew into a much more enjoyable stay. I didn't know anything at all about sports, so I wasn't much help there. You'd be amazed to hear the variety of interesting subjects 30 captive young men in the same room can come up with. Arguments were sort of pointless, since nobody could reach anybody else to fight it out.

My parents and my brothers and sisters came to visit me often, with my dad coming every single weekend that I was there. It was a 120 mile one-way trip for him on two lane roads and it touched me deeply that he would do that for me. He'd also bring my girlfriend, Miss B, so his visits were highly anticipated.

We'd have Marine officers, including Generals, come to visit, usually on Mondays, and it was gratifying to meet and talk with the men who led Divisions and still cared enough to take the time out to come talk to us.

On one visit, Major General Lewis Fields told me that he'd looked into my record and saw that I had been a Lance Corporal for 18 months and he asked if I was a "s__tbird". I indignantly told him that I wasn't, that "they just forgot about me." I don't know – maybe they forgot about me because I was a s__tbird, but I was proud enough of myself, anyway. The next day, he came by and promoted me to Corporal.

I even got a visit from Lieutenant General Victor "The Brute" Krulak, who hit his head on the edge of my traction rig. I told him that we needed to put a "rotating red beacon on that thing – you're the third General Officer today to hit his head on it." That was a bad move. You have NEVER been chewed out unless you were chewed out by the Brute. I learned that I could lie rigidly at attention.

The battle between us and the nurses continued. Every single morning, they'd wake us at 0530 and the student Corpsmen would come into the ward, and they would train them how to start IVs, take blood, etc., on all of us— both arms. Those new Corpsmen were an untalented bunch and every day we had missed veins, arteries squirting, bones nicked, and needles bent into us. Our arms looked like heroin addicts' with a bad aim. Our nurses laughed at our complaints and said, "look at the big, bad Marines who aren't afraid of bullets but are scared of little bitty needles." That was annoying.

Nurse L was the Head Nurse and as always, she introduced herself by pointing at the Lieutenant Commander's stripes on her hat and telling us that she was an officer. She developed a habit of waking us for our morning needlefest by whipping off our blankets in our unheated ward. I passed the word to everyone later that night to take their pants off under their blankets. Nurse L knew that there was a conspiracy by the time she ripped away blanket #4 and saw yet another naked young man. The practice of removing blankets as a method for holding reveille was stopped.

I went through several operations to graft new skin over the holes in my leg. They took the skin for the grafts from the front of my left leg which eventually closed off the open part but left me with two sore legs at once. Bit by bit, over the months, the pain dropped off and despite being fully anchored to my bed, a surprising amount of freedom was possible. I went from Demerol (which we referred to as "Mr. Demerol" by us) to Darvon which seemed to be less effective than aspirin, but I suppose it was designed to lessen the chances of addiction. I talked one of the Corpsmen into giving me a crutch, which I hid between my mattresses. He didn't ask me what I needed it for, though I'm sure that question went through his mind. I waited until the nurses were off duty (about 6:30 in the evening) and the duty Corpsman went to sleep (usually 8:30 or so) and then I pulled that crutch out and I used it to pole me and my bed away from the ward and down the central hall. I'd visit the snack bar vending machines, call my girlfriend on the pay phone and sometimes visit other wards to look for my friends. Before daybreak, I'd gondola my bed back in place and nobody was the wiser.

I thought. Soon, several others in my ward got crutches and when evening rolled around, beds were traveling up and down the halls, like ghost ships prowling the sea. The most popular place to visit was the ladies' ward. Eventually, we got caught: one guy poled his way outdoors down a ramp and then couldn't get back up the ramp, so he was right out there in the open when the nurses came on duty. Most people have no idea how inventive young men can be when not watched carefully.

I had a small Japanese-made black and white TV of my own as many of the guys did and daytime TV in the mid-'60s was horrible: bad cartoons, lame game shows, and soap operas. What I wanted to watch were the evening shows, the news, movies, documentaries but we had to shut the TVs off at 8:00 sharp. Needless to say, I'd try to watch TV later and developed a way of doing it. I'd turn the sound way down (no earplugs in those days) and I'd darken the screen, so it barely showed and then watch whatever I wanted. But one evening Nurse L was working late and I heard her loud footsteps heading toward our ward. I quickly reduced the sound to zero and darkened the screen – but didn't turn it off because they took a while to warm up in those days. Nurse L walked past me and then stopped. She walked up to me and shook my shoulder to wake me (since I was pretending to be asleep) and she said "Forrest – why is there a light on in the back of your TV?"

Thinking fast, I said, "Pilot light, Ma'am" and I think that she would have accepted that answer if everyone didn't start laughing. She rolled my TV to her office for that night.

Men healed up and left the ward, new people were rolled in to replace them and the ward was a home of sorts for all of us. We had a daily routine of tests and treatments and doses and sometimes surgeries but the life in the ward remained friendly and sometimes entertaining. The young guys there were from all over and everyone had their stories. One guy had been riding "shotgun" for a Combat Engineer dump truck when a burst of fire hit him in both sides of the chest and killed the driver. The truck rolled down an embankment and flipped on its side, throwing him out of the truck on the ground, the driver's body over his. The VC came to the wreck and checked him and driver out to see if they were dead. He held absolutely still while the VC went through his pockets and took his watch, then one of the enemy put a rifle up to his leg and fired. He was able to suppress his reaction and they still thought he was dead – then a burst of fire hit the VC squad and the squad of Marines that killed them found him and "flagged down" a passing Huey helicopter to get him to the hospital. He did lose that leg while we were there.

Another Marine, "Tex" (who I knew from Boot Camp, but he was never anywhere near Texas – he just liked to be called "Tex") was blown up when his truck drove over a large mine and besides the broken legs and hips he got, he also got an elaborately powder burned face that resembled Maori tattoos. It was like all of his facial features were in permanent shadow, from the bottom up and honestly, it improved him.

At some point, a Marine was brought into the ward who had some broken bones and very badly burned hands – they looked like curved, black claws and he had an armed MP guarding him. Later at night, I asked him why he had a guard and he told me that he was going to be court-martialed for murdering his Captain after he recovered. He said that he had been a crewman aboard a CH-46 helicopter and the captain was an officer who didn't fly often, preferring more administrative duties and according to him had a reputation for cowardice among the troops. They were flying fairly high up when they were hit, and the engines started to burn. CH-46s burned easily and enthusiastically, so the crew in the back yelled over the interphones to hurry up and get down on the ground as fast as possible. The Captain ignored them, preferring I guess to get farther into friendlier territory before landing. The fire raced forward inside the aircraft and one by one, the men in back burned up. Finally, the Marine said, he was burning, and the helicopter finally hit the ground, hard, and he tumbled out. The Captain was untouched but when he exited the cabin, the Marine said he pulled his pistol and killed him—the last thing he would ever do with those hands. He was moved within a few days, and I never learned his name or what happened to him.

Another helicopter crewman was brought into the ward who told me that he was up for the Medal of Honor. He told me that he was on a medevac flight and as the Marines were carrying casualties to his helicopter, they were hit by a burst of gunfire and the stretcher bearers were all wounded and down. He said that he couldn't traverse his machine gun far enough over to suppress the enemy fire, so he ran out of the helicopter to try to get the casualties himself. He told me that he was shot five times, covering one of the men with his body, like a human flak jacket to protect him. He was moved soon, and I never found out his name (or I just can't remember it) and I don't know if he ever got an award. It certainly sounded like he deserved it.

When the run-up to the 1968 Tet Offensive began, we received the first casualties from battles near Hue City and one of them came from my artillery battery, Bravo 1/11. He described the ambushed convoy he had been in, remembering in exact sequence of who had been hit and where. He told me that the convoy commander had been killed by over 15 shots and that the only reason the survivors lived was because an army administrative unit manning a pair of "Duster" tracked 40mm twin-barreled antiaircraft guns came to their rescue and overwhelmed the enemy attackers long enough for them to pile the survivors on the engine decks and back them out of there.

We occasionally got entertainers to visit us in the ward and the ones I remember were Nancy Sinatra (a very personable lady who gave us pictures of herself in a bikini), Carole Burnett (very warm and attentive), and Jim Nabors (a really nice guy). I guess that there weren't a lot of people that came in to see us but those few that went to all that trouble were deeply appreciated.

I was feeling a lot better, and I was sure that I could just undo my traction rig and just walk out of there. No pain at all now but my doctor – that same humorless Dr. K – insisted that I still had a ways to go. My family visited often and one time that I remember the best was when my dad brought several sisters and brothers, and they essentially flooded the place. My oldest sister was 17 at the time and she was very popular with the guys of the ward. At some point, my sister came to me crying and she told me that one of the Marines grabbed her chest and held her. This Marine was somebody I knew from his prior visits to the ward, PFC R – and shortly after I had calmed my sister down and she had gone to find Dad, PFC R came into our ward and sat in a chair about three feet to my left. Worse, he bragged about "copping a feel" on my sister and smirked at me.

He should have paid attention to what I was doing: I had been building a small model plane on a lap tray and I had just dumped all of the parts on my lap. With my right hand, I pulled myself up using the grab handle on the traction rig, then I swung out towards PFC R's chair and pulled his chair towards me. Then I swung that metal tray into his face hard enough to bend it into a "V." He started to stand, and I hit him again going in the other direction to the back of his head, more or less bending the tray back straight. He stood up, howling with anger and came at me. I hit him with the full contents of my piss pot and soaked him from head to waist.

Now he spluttered with dripping rage and started to come after me and just that second, Nurse L grabbed him in a hammerlock and yelled: "don't you dare hurt that poor wounded man!" I was starting to like Nurse L. She was fun.

In late December 1967, I was measured for a steel leg brace that would fit from my hip bone to my foot, attached to one of my dress shoes. They detached all of my traction rigging and attached a drill motor to that pin in my leg and just undrilled it right out (there was a burr on the pin from the cutting, so it "rifled" the hole in my leg). They put the brace on me, attaching the leather straps and I carefully swung my lower body off the bed and with help from Corpsman "Ski," carefully began to stand. I was finally there, standing – free of the bed, free of the network of pulleys and ropes, free of that pin in my leg!

But I started to feel lightheaded and then dizzier, and I told Ski that I was going to faint. Ski was one of those navy Corpsmen who was even more gung-ho than any Marine and he even had a high-and-tight Marine haircut, so he told me with a growl "you're not going to faint; keep trying." I looked at him intently and then fainted. I came to in my bed and realized that it was going to take a step-by-step process to build up my strength and my heart again to get back to the vertical world. One of the funniest memories of when I first stood was when Nurse L came up to me and looked up into my eyes and said softly: "Rick – you're so tall!" OK, so maybe I won't melt that nurse's statue after all.

I was told by Dr. K that I'd never walk well again but I did learn to walk well. He told me that there was no way that I'd ever run again but after a couple of years, I did run again. I think that doctors are taught to tell young guys like I was that something isn't possible, just so we'd try harder to make it possible.

I wasn't entirely done with the hospital, though: as an "ambulatory" patient, you were put to work in the ward, cleaning and mopping and helping out. Dr. K had me photograph him during his operations to record his work.

I was allowed to go on liberty up to home near Los Angeles now and my khaki uniform flapped like a flag in the breeze on me because I only weighed 106 pounds at that point (compared to the 175 pounds I weighed when I was hit and I'm 5 foot 10, no matter how tall Nurse L thought I was). I got dropped off at the San Clemente Gate and then I tried to hitchhike from there to L.A.

I stood out there on the freeway onramp for hours, with my leg brace and crutches. Cars would slow by me, look at me, give the Peace sign (two upraised fingers in a V) and then flip me a center finger. Finally, some young guy in a red MGB sports car showed up and asked where I was going, then told me to get in. Easier said than done: my right leg was a straight, steel-reinforced plank and the Brits designed that car for little-bitty Brit midgets or double amputees. After a lot of sweat and struggling, I finally got in and stowed my crutches next to me.

We rode quietly down the road for about ten or twenty miles and the young man driving asked me how I broke my leg. I told him that I got shot. He asked me "where?"; so I pointed at the center of my right thigh. He said: "no – what country?"

I said "Vietnam" and he rapidly slowed his car and then stopped on the edge of the freeway and said, "get out." I struggled again to get out of that little car, and he left, and I was alone there, with cars racing past me. You would probably wonder why I didn't lose my temper and punch that guy or chew him out, but I was so shocked by what he did that I was silent and got right out of his car. I crutched myself to the next off ramp and then hitched a ride back to Camp Pendleton and the hospital. I was exhausted and I hurt again, so, so much for my first liberty. My next liberty went better, and I was able to get all the way to my girlfriend's house in Burbank. I traveled in civilian clothes this time, so I didn't run into any trouble. I guess everyone thought I was hurt doing something worthwhile, like playing football maybe. I enjoyed my liberty a bit too long, so when I got started hitchhiking in Burbank it was 0200 and I was running very late to get to the L.A. bus station and then back to Camp Pendleton Hospital by 0600.

I stood on that Lankershim Boulevard corner for a while and absolutely nobody came by, hostile or not. Then a police officer passed me once, and then came back and turned his red lights on and stopped next to me. He got out and asked me what I was doing there. It's hard to imagine what kinds of crooks hang out at street corners with crutches and wearing a steel leg brace, but I'm not a highly trained law enforcement officer. After I showed him my I.D. and told him that I was trying to get to the bus station, he had me get into his car and drove me a few blocks to where another police car was parked – a long, low LAPD freeway cruiser. As we pulled into the parking lot, a young woman got out of the cruiser and was clearly getting herself decent, buttoning her blouse and trying to stay inconspicuous. The first cop talked to the cruiser cop and then he told me to get into the cruiser. We got up on the freeway and this new cop was a large, wide-faced casual sort of guy and he asked me questions about what I was doing in Burbank and then about my part of the war and my injuries. Then he said: "Aw, screw it – you won't make it back in time" and picked up speed rapidly (there was a large speedometer above the center of his dash) up to 125 mph and kept it there, red lights on, and occasionally hitting the siren to chase away anyone in our path. It was a little disconcerting that he drove the whole way with one hand on the steering wheel while facing me, asking questions – but we didn't hit anybody. He drove me the whole 120 miles to the front door of the hospital, God bless him.

A week or so before Christmas, I was transferred to Support Company, 14 Area, Camp Pendleton, which was an artificial unit where they parked the recovering wounded as well as men getting out of the brig. Kind of shows you what esteem our Marine Corps had for us. The bunch of us recent escapees from the hospital were being evaluated to see whether the Marine Corps would keep us in or discharge us. The "Brig Rats" were in that same barracks to await their next assignment or more likely awaiting some sort of less-than-honorable discharge and we were at their mercy. They stole us blind and there was very little we could do about it. The recovering wounded were missing limbs, or like me in braces with crutches, or missing an eye; that sort of thing where the Brig Rats were, well, physically fit criminals. They stole everything I owned, including the pathetic few souvenirs that I still had and when the Marine Corps gave me a document to go and get fitted for more uniforms, they stole those too after I got them.

We were used for slave labor, as it seemed that the Marine Corps considered us little better than malingerers, for all that wonderful bed time we had had. Our company commander was a Captain S, a ramrod-straight, shaved-headed athlete who hadn't been to Vietnam and clearly resented us for our having been there. He used to have us fall out for formation every Saturday morning for inspection before he would approve any liberty. Liberty, if we got it, was from noon Saturday until 6:00 PM Sunday and since we were still located in the bowels of that very large base that was a long way from any fun stuff, we were limited in dwell time. Standing in formation was torture for us because wherever we had been injured still hurt. I clearly remember one of my fellow Marines starting to bleed from a leg wound that reopened while we were standing there while Capt. S slowly moved down the ranks inspecting our haircuts and uniforms. I helped that guy get back to the barracks and helped him stop the bleeding. He went back to the hospital.

The "slave labor" we were farmed out to was everything from grass mowing to cutting up the pervasive ice plants (which are quite heavy: they're filled with water) to pulling butts (targets) at the Regimental Rifle Range. That last one was really great fun for us recovering victims of bullet wounds. What could possibly be more invigorating than hearing that high-pitched crack of bullets hitting targets just above our heads, over and over? After all, it's exactly the same sound those bullets made hitting us. I remember shaking violently for a while afterward.

Another fun duty was serving as a chaplain's assistant during the weekends. That was despised because it meant that you had to work weekends, helping the chapel crew change the chapel over from Jewish services to Protestant to Catholic to accommodate those different faiths. Easy enough duty, just no fun.

My sergeant in charge of me called me in and told me that I was assigned to Chaplain Assistant duty for three weekends in a row, Christmas, New Year's, and the weekend after. I told him that that was crazy – I hadn't been home for leave for a while – and Christmas? I said that I'd happily do one, just pick one but why all three? He just told me to do it, since that meant nobody else would have to be stuck.

It's a little-known fact outside the Marine Corps, that every Marine, no matter how lowly in rank, has the absolute right to see the Commanding General and have his case heard. It's called Request Mast and you do have to go through your Chain of Command step by step, but you cannot be denied that right.

So, I requested mast to see our Platoon Commander, a very new Second Lieutenant who I had only seen around once before, and he listened patiently to me and nodded. So, I requested mast to the next step in the chain, Captain S. As I mentioned before, he didn't like us and he bristled with barely restrained fury at the gall I had, coming to see him with my sniveling complaints. Further, he didn't like my haircut.

So, then I requested mast to see the Battalion Commander. Needless to say, Capt. S's face turned even redder, and he went from furious to hopping mad but even he couldn't deny me that right. He was sure that the Colonel would take care of me, so he hissed his approval and tossed me out of his office.

As far as I knew, I had never seen much less met the Battalion Commander, but I was grimly ready to face him. I arrived at the appointed time and was ushered into his office, a wood-paneled affair with crossed US and Marine flags behind him. He received me with stern silence while I told him of the situation and my disagreement with it. He told me to sit in a chair along the far wall of the room and told me to keep my mouth shut. I sat in that chair, and I saw him speak with the Sergeant Major for a few seconds and then return to writing something on papers on his desk. After a half hour's silent wait, Captain S, the lieutenant Platoon Commander, and my sergeant all entered the Colonel's office in smart precision and stood three across at the center of the Colonel's desk. I noted with hope that the Captain was carrying the duty logbook.

The Colonel asked Capt. S why this Marine – pointing towards me – had duty at the chapel three weekends in a row, since he noted that the logbook only showed one different person per each weekend. Captain S told him that: "it's a new program, Sir – we're implementing it now; so that once a Marine has served those three weekends in a row, he'll never have the duty again." Considering that none of us would every spend more than maybe six weeks in Support Company, that was ridiculous, and I wanted to say so, but I kept my mouth shut.

The Colonel told Captain S: "Why, that's excellent – I like innovation" and Captain S beamed but he said, "instead of that Marine trying it out, I want you three to have that duty; Christmas, New Year's, and the weekend after instead and when you're finished, I want you to come back to me and tell me how it was, OK?" "You're dismissed," he said, and they filed out.

The Colonel had me stand in front of his desk and said: "you don't remember me, do you? I used to come to your ward in the hospital every Monday to see how you were doing. It's really great to see you standing there." He called in the Sergeant Major and in a little impromptu ceremony, promoted me to sergeant and gave me orders to the Marine Corps Air Station in Tustin, California, so I could be closer to my family.

The Marine Corps in those days had its problems but justice could be had. I remembered the results of my only Request Mast through my long career in the Marines and I always made sure I listened and did the best I could for my troops when they came to me, asking for help.

Recovery and the Effects of War

I WAS TRANSFERRED TO A HELICOPTER TRAINING SQUADRON – HMMT-302 – and had a good year working with the air wing and recovering. The Air Wing didn't know exactly what to do with me, a "grunt" (to the Air Wing, everyone who wasn't one of them was a grunt) but I made myself useful as a Duty Driver, a brig "chaser" (prisoner escort/guard), a mail room clerk, a Platoon Sergeant, and an instructor for training Marines to fire the .50 caliber machine gun from CH-46 helicopters. I was discharged from the Marine Corps exactly four years to the day I entered boot camp, so the Marine Corps got every ounce out me that they could.

I got a job at Lockheed Aircraft in Burbank. I started college again as an Engineering Major, and I tried my best to blend back into a normal young life, but it wasn't completely possible. I had a lot of pain from my still-injured leg, I deeply resented the American public for turning against us and I positively despised men of my age who had stayed home. I drank a lot. I got married to that young lady who my dad brought to the hospital almost every weekend, which turned out to be a really bad thing because she was very young and had no patience at all with my war-induced idiosyncrasies and did not want to listen to anything about my time in the Marines. That marriage did not last. I would flinch and even throw myself to the ground every time I heard a loud bang. The guys at Lockheed thought it was great fun to drop a piece of sheet steel on the hard floor behind me and when I flinched at the noise, they'd yell— "hit the deck, hit the deck!" and laugh.

Ah, great fun.

I had bad dreams for a long time, the most common being hearing a small sound, then a slightly louder sound. Then a bang. Then a very loud bang and

I would fall on the floor, out of bed trying to escape the sound. I would be very watchful all the time, scanning the horizon or if I was in a building like a store, watching all around me.

I'd see a funny commercial on TV and laugh and then start crying for the young men I knew who would never see that commercial like I could. I couldn't stand to be in crowds – I'd get frantic and even violent if I was hemmed in.

It took me a long time to measure the effects of my experience in Vietnam on me and those around me. I was changed but I think that most of it was for the better. I knew at least that I could survive and endure in very rigorous and dangerous situations. It helped a lot to have Cpl. A, and some of the other guys who made it with us get together and drink beer and talk. We supported each other through a difficult time. It did not help that Hollywood relished making ridiculous, cartoon-like movies and TV shows which showed Vietnam Veterans go violently crazy and begin murdering in all directions (*Rambo, Billy Jack, et al.*) or pathetic cliche-filled and insulting junk like *Apocalypse Now, the Deer Hunter, or Platoon*. It was standard fare when we got back and the only thing that was offered except for the equally silly and unrealistic (but at least favorable) John Wayne epic, *the Green Berets*. Part of it was, that Producers, Directors and Writers, had little or no experience with Vietnam or combat, or even military service and since most of them leaned left, there was no motivation to get the story straight. There was never any attempt at all to make a movie about us or our war realistic or sympathetic. Quite a long time after our war, the movie *We were soldiers then and Young* came out and while also more or less favorable of us in its storyline, it had the usual "napalm grenades," spurious sound effects and it was obviously filmed in California – something even my wife noticed – it didn't look at all like Vietnam.

I need to mention too, that our loving government – specifically, the Air Force – spent nearly every day of the entire war, spraying chemicals over all of the jungled portions of South Vietnam to "defoliate" the trees to make the enemy more visible for them. Two things apparently never crossed their minds:

When you remove the jungle cover, the enemy can see you better too – and their antiaircraft fire became more accurate and the regions from the mountains to the borders with Laos and Cambodia are littered with American aircraft aluminum and as yet unfound remains of our aircrews.

The garbage they were spraying was insanely poisonous, and it spread downstream in the previously-mentioned rainfall into the streams and the rivers, the same streams and rivers where we insignificant ground troops and the Vietnamese civilians we were there to protect got our drinking water – and there was no filtration system on Earth that could remove that poison.

All of us who served in Vietnam have that poison in our bodies. Nearly every single man suffered from a number of horrific diseases after Vietnam which was linked to Agent Orange exposure.

After a while, a long while, I began to forgive the men who did not go to Vietnam with us. It's hard to blame someone for the decisions they make when they're 18, 19, 20 years old. You take a path and the path branches, and you pick a branch. Whatever branch you picked was the right one because there is no going back.

I still haven't forgiven the "antiwar" activists who met with the enemy and helped them fight us. They had a regular commuter service going back and forth from the States to Hanoi and for some unfathomable reason, our government didn't do anything at all to them.

On point of fact, our government was pretty well missing in action throughout our war. There were no serious attempts to speak to the American people to explain why we were in Vietnam and what we were doing, no serious attempts to rally the people behind our mission, no attempts at all to help us returning vets adjust to our new realities. The whole focus of the government's information dissemination was the weekly "body count" totals which showed how many VC we supposedly killed versus the total number of our soldiers and Marines who were killed, as if it was a football score. The Veteran's Administration was a sad joke; they were completely unavailable by phone, replied to letters only reluctantly and didn't offer any services to help us. The sole program that I did get help with was the GI Bill but that only paid a small part of my college tuition. The only funny moment with the VA was the week I was separating from the Marine Corps, all of us who were being discharged were addressed in an auditorium on the El Toro Marine Base and the VA representative asked, "how many of you have been wounded?" and we stayed quiet. Then he asked, "OK. How many of you were hurt" and again, nothing. Then he said "OK. How many of you have been shot?" and a whole bunch of hands went up and he said, "you Marines drive me crazy!" Now, a long time after our war, the VA is a greatly improved and more responsive organization but back then, it was an almost opaque wall to us.

The enemy sympathizers brought back propaganda and of all things, movies and I remember seeing that "peace movies" were being shown in our campus theater at California State University, Northridge, one day. I went in the campus theater, and I saw that they were showing the movie *"Day of the Plane Hunt,"* a North Vietnamese military documentary showing their antiaircraft crews shooting down our planes. Each time a plane fell, burning, the audience of students would stand and cheer. Each time a shocked and injured American pilot was shown captured at bayonet point, the audience cheered. Tables near the theater were covered with enemy literature and propaganda posters, most of it printed in Hanoi and brought back by the so-called antiwar (but really pro-enemy) activists.

Demonstrators at Cal State Northridge in 1970. Note the two Vietcong flags. (Photo from Author's Collection)

I wonder what World War II vets would have thought if Americans at home showed enemy movies and cheered at the loss or imprisonment of their compatriots or even better, held demonstrations against that war and carried the Japanese or the Nazi flags. Yet, somehow, we Vietnam Veterans were expected to just accept all of that and "move on."

We did, no thanks to the rest of our country back then.

NSA SPEAKERS BUREAU

THE DELEGATION OF AMERICAN STUDENT LEADERS THAT NEGOTIATED THE PEACE TREATY WITH THE STUDENTS OF VIETNAM ARE AVILABLE FOR SPEAKING ENGAGEMENTS THROUGH THE USNSA SPEAKERS BUREAU. IN ADDITION, PEOPLE LIKE RENNIE DAVIS DAVID DELLINGER, JOHN FROINES, BETTY FRIEDAN, BARBARA SEAMAN, SAM LOVE, ERIC SCHNAPPER, MEMBERS OF THE SEATTLE SEVEN, AND NUMEROUS OTHER ACTIVISTS AND RESOURCE PEOPLE CAN BE BOOKED THROUGH THE NSA SPEAKERS BUREAU. FOR MORE INFORMATION WRITE TO DREW OLIM AT 2II5 S STREET N.W., WASHINGTON, D.C. 20008 OR CALL 387-7700.

(PICTURED BELOW IS PHAM VAN DONG (CENTER, FIRST ROW) AND DAVID IFSHIN (TO THE IMMEDIATE RIGHT OF PHAM) AS WELL AS THE OTHER MEMBERS OF THE DELEGATION AND SOME OF THE MANY VIETNAMESE THEY MET IN THE NORTH.)

How is this not treason? Smiling Americans meeting with North Vietnamese leaders in 1969. "NSA" stood for National Student's Association, not the spy agency with the same initials. (Photo from the Author's collection)

We even had some alleged Vietnam Vets campaigning against the war (the "Vietnam Veterans Against the War (VVAW)") but very few of them seemed to be the real thing. I had one alleged army Vietnam Veteran ask me if I had "ever raped anybody." I told him that no, I hadn't. So, he said "if you never raped anybody then you weren't in combat." It's hard to fathom anybody that would say something like that. I was so tightly wired in combat that the last thing on earth that would have occurred to me would be to attack some woman. The object was to stay alive and in one piece – it never crossed my mind to try to have sex with some woman, particularly the poor, skinny peasant women with stained black teeth from a lifetime of chewing betel nuts we saw in the field. Shows you the kind of ridiculous, posturing blowhards we used to meet.

Eventually, I healed. I was able to bend my knee almost to 90 degrees and then started to run again. The Marine Corps sent me a letter asking if I would be interested in an officer candidate program and I was most certainly interested. I was tired of civilian life and the strangeness of our country back then and I wanted to get back into our war. I was commissioned a Lieutenant on April Fool's Day 1973 and in 1975 almost made it back to Vietnam as part of the force trying to hold the perimeter around Saigon but our plane was turned around to Guam while the NVA rocketed Tan Son Nhut airport and then I flew to Okinawa and boarded a ship and we sailed to Vietnam as it fell to the enemy. I spent another 23 years in the Marines, eventually commanding an artillery battalion in California.

I have always hated parades, those military parades where we would stand for hours, rifles at our sides or sword in hand, waiting for an order that would give us some kind of movement. Partially it was because my leg hurt and partially because it was all meaningless: the Marine Corps doesn't exist for parades, or flags, or wildly exaggerated stories or padded histories or teary-eyed remembrances. The Marine Corps exists to kill people or to be killed in the process of killing people (or at least sometimes, scare our potential enemies enough that they don't want to fight us). Sometimes we get more of them and sometimes they get more of us. We don't run away, we don't hide, we rarely use any elegance, but we fight. We fight for our country, we fight because we are ordered to, and mostly we fight for each other. It has been that way for a couple of centuries and with luck, it will continue for as long as we are needed and there are still men (and women) left to do it.

I am happy with the branch of life that I took. I served in tough circumstances with the best young men our country had. I learned that I could stay up with them and I learned so much from all of them. I learned that like the many others who served in Vietnam with me, I was willing to give my life if needed to protect our country and a people who need our help. I thank God every day that I'm here and able to discern the gifts that I have been given.

I'll always be proud of the men and the families of those men who served along with me in our war.

I have been asked a lot of times "if it was all worth it?" That's very hard to answer. On one hand, we lost tens of thousands of completely irreplaceable young men and wrecked many tens of thousands of families in the process. We saw our country turn against us and what we were trying to do and, in some cases, actively conduct acts of terror at home and supported our enemies while we were still fighting them. In the end, we watched our country give up completely and then turn their backs on the millions of people who had risked everything they had to be on our side. For me, it was a cruel awakening about who we were as a nation and what we actually valued. While we went through the misery of living away from home in a hot, tropical, alien country with constant fear and sometimes losing parts of our bodies or even our young lives, America acted as though we didn't exist (or worse, as if we were the enemy) and they went on with football games, and television shows and building careers and families— sacrificing nothing as if there wasn't any war at all going on. Our nation continued its expensive "Space Race" to the moon, continued with the Civil Rights/War on Poverty programs, continued to support Israel in its fights with its Arab neighbors (1967, 1973), continued funding the intense needs of the Cold War in Europe and we and our war were almost an afterthought and we felt disposable, like Kleenex. We were, after all, just "somebody else's children."

But despite all of this, we held on in Vietnam. For the long ten years from 1965 to 1975, the world saw us fight hard and effectively. It was obvious to anyone paying attention that the only reason we were fighting was because we had an ally being overwhelmed by a massive communist effort and that we few Americans with a handful of Australians, South Koreans, and Filipinos were overcoming everything as it came at us. We weren't there to gain a colony. We weren't there to take over the country. We weren't there to annex the fifty-first through fifty-fourth states.

We weren't there for any economic gain – we spent trillions of dollars. We were there to save a people from the massive worldwide effort to overcome their – and our – freedom.

The enemy had no chance at all of winning if we had kept going and they knew it. Their main method of dealing with us was to keep the attrition of our young men going and to influence the American people behind us and it worked.

Yet, a few years later the Cold War was over. The sides at the negotiating tables had a different view of America's strength because they had seen us fighting a long-distance war with courage, skill, and determination. We weren't the weaklings they thought we were, and, in the end, it was that view that finally convinced our adversaries that we were more than strong enough. In the popular view, Vietnam was a loss but the vision of us "soft and comfortable" Americans fighting it out in the heat and torrential rain and misery remained in the view of our enemies and our allies. We showed that we had steel in us and in the end, that was the view that has remained in the eyes of the world as the American legacy of the Vietnam War.

UNITED STATES MARINE CORPS
HEADQUARTERS, FLEET MARINE FORCE, PACIFIC
FPO, SAN FRANCISCO 96610

In the name of the President of the United States, the Commanding General, Fleet Marine Force, Pacific takes pleasure in presenting the BRONZE STAR MEDAL to

LANCE CORPORAL FORREST RICHARD LINDSEY

UNITED STATES MARINE CORPS

for service as set forth in the following

CITATION:

"For heroic achievement in connection with operations against insurgent communist (Viet Cong) forces in the Republic of Vietnam while serving as a Scout with an Artillery Forward Observer Team attached to Company G, Second Battalion, First Marines, First Marine Division. On 13 May 1967, while on patrol near Dien Ban in Quang Nam Province, Lance Corporal LINDSEY's unit came under intense enemy small arms fire. Repeatedly exposing himself to enemy fire, he ably assisted in adjusting artillery fire on the enemy. Observing two wounded Marines lying in an open area, he unhesitatingly and with complete disregard for his own safety, maneuvered through heavy enemy small arms fire to aid his injured comrades. With the assistance of another Marine, he successfully moved one Marine to relative safety. While fearlessly maneuvering through the hostile fire to the assistance of the second Marine, Lance Corporal LINDSEY was seriously wounded by enemy fire and was unable to continue. His courageous actions and aggressive fighting spirit undoubtedly saved the life of one wounded Marine and were an inspiration to all who observed him. Lance Corporal LINDSEY's courage, bold initiative and selfless devotion to duty were in keeping with the highest traditions of the Marine Corps and of the United States Naval Service."

Lance Corporal LINDSEY is authorized to wear the Combat "V".

FOR THE PRESIDENT,

V. H. KRULAK
LIEUTENANT GENERAL, U. S. MARINE CORPS
COMMANDING

TEMPORARY CITATION

Epilogue 1

The author as a Second Lieutenant waiting on Okinawa for the word to go back to Vietnam in 1975. (Photo from the Author's Collection)

In 1975, I had been a Marine lieutenant for two years and I was assigned to the 1st Marine Brigade and I was currently a "G-4B" (Assistant Logistics Officer) at Brigade Headquarters and watched our war steadily go downhill. I read the daily Intelligence Summaries and it was obvious that the combination of us pulling out of Vietnam, the resignation of President Nixon, and then the ending of funding the South Vietnamese government would result in an enemy victory. I was overwhelmed with sadness that we as a country were giving up after all we and the South Vietnamese had done and lost during those long years.

In the middle of the night, I was recalled by my parent unit, the 1st Bn, 12th Marines and told to come straight into the battalion commander's office. I went in as told and as an afterthought, brought my own personal .45 with me. My instincts were good, and I was put on a plane with three enlisted men to go from Hawaii to Guam and we three were to be a Naval gunfire Spot team to be sent in to Vung Tau to direct the ship's fire against the North Vietnamese who were heading in an unstoppable wave towards Saigon. While we were in Guam, our mission changed, and we were to become part of another Marine Force to land at Tan Son Nhut and then become part of an antitank element to be sent to Saigon and form part of the defense of Saigon near a sports stadium. One of the lieutenants in the unit told the troops during an instruction period that "we didn't have a chance" against the NVA T-54s and T-55s and that we should fire a token shot and then escape. I interrupted that lieutenant (I somewhat haughtily referred to the new lieutenants that joined after 1972 as "draft dodgers" because they decided to become Marine officers after the war was essentially over) and told the troops that we would have adequate weapons (105mm howitzers firing High Explosive, Plastic Tracer (HEP-T)) and to aim at the point where the turret and the hull met and that would kill the tank. I told them that we were absolutely required to stand our ground and kill tanks "because there was nobody behind us and everyone was counting on us." Behind us there wouldn't be anyone able to stop a tank, so we would have to do it.

I also told them that we could also fall back on the "Marine Corps method" of stopping a tank. One of the troops asked what the "Marine Corps method" was, and I told him that it was to stop the lead tank and demand to see the tank driver's license. "If he wasn't fully rated for the 50-ton T-54, throw his a__ out." That lightened the mood somewhat.

As we flew towards Tan Son Nhut, we were turned back to Guam because the airfield was under enemy rocket fire and it was considered too dangerous to land. Our mission was scrubbed, and we flew to Okinawa and then after some waiting there, I was put on the USS Dubuque and watched the war collapse from there.

I was deeply ashamed that we didn't hold the enemy off long enough to take all of those who helped us, and we left them for the enemy's mercies which were few enough. They faced "reeducation camps" for years, even decades, or escaped as "boat people" to our country and other countries or they were simply murdered. It was a sad and shameful end to the one really generous and courageous thing that we as country had done to rescue good people from a vicious and merciless enemy.

Epilogue 2

IN 2000, MY WIFE AND I TRAVELED TO VIETNAM AS TOURISTS SO I could show her what the places I worked in and fought for were like and for me to see what happened there and see how the Vietnamese were doing. We landed in Danang, of all things, and my nerves were up all the way from Bangkok. I was actually shaking when I approached the Vietnamese guard to show our passports – he was wearing that damned NVA pith helmet and he had the red collar tabs and all I saw was our old enemy up very close. (I had previously confronted that uniform in 1990 when I was an On-Site Inspection Agency Team Leader in the Soviet Union. When we were shunted through Sheremetyevo airport, I went up an escalator and ran face to face with an NVA officer and I was shocked and frozen in position, but the young Vietnamese officer just looked at me like: "what's the matter with you?" He hadn't been born yet when I was fighting people that looked just like him.) But the guard didn't even bother looking at us and boredly passed us through and once we were past him, I felt this huge wave of relief as I was once again on the streets of Danang. Nothing looked any different except there were many, many more Honda 50 type motorbikes on the streets and there wasn't as much dust everywhere. The colors looked clearer. No one paid much attention to us as we visited Phu Bai and Hue and Khe Sanh and Quang Tri. Everything had changed but the South Vietnamese were still running stores and open markets in their usual capitalist fashion (the Southerners are excellent businessmen) and they were thrilled to see free-spending Americans. We bought a huge quantity of candy and bubble blowers for the kids and the kids, as always, followed us around in large, happy groups. Towards the end of our week-long tour, our guide consented to take us to Hill 55 and the Bravo Battery position and to the villages where we patrolled and where I was wounded. A lot had changed: the rice fields were smaller due to growth of the size of the villages and our old battery position was now a Chinese-style graveyard with colorful family tombs. Hill 55 had a large concrete statue of a Vietcong trooper on it as a memorial and none of the villagers paid much attention to us as they went about their work. We went to Xuan Diem and looked for the place where I had been shot and I think that I found it but was hard to tell, since the tree lines and the fields had changed over time. We ran into a woman named "Annie" who had sold us sodas when she was a little girl and she still spoke some '60s English ("No sweat, man"). Annie came with us to An Trach, and we saw that the Catholic Church that had been destroyed in 1966 had been rebuilt. We met the parish priest Father D, who did not speak English or French, so Annie translated for us. I told Father what had happened there – the church had been used as a machine gun position for the VC and we had just about blown it flat – so I was surprised and pleased to see the Saint Joseph the Worker Church there now. Father D asked me if I could buy them a tractor and I asked him why. He said that they needed a tractor so that all the farmers in the area could plow their fields with it instead of using the water buffalos. Because they had to use the buffalos, the kids couldn't go to school because they're the ones that tend buffalos. I promised that we would get the money to him, and we did, thanks to the Catholic and Protestant congregations at the Quantico Marine Base Chapel. We wired the money to him and his villagers within a week. I have the photo of Father D and his tractor now.

Father D and his tractor. (Photo from the Author's Collection)

I tried to find the former VC whose finger and edge of hand I had shot off and who had helped me get on the helicopter but no one we spoke to knew him. They said that: "he must have been from another area." It's a shame – I would love to have taken him and his family to dinner.

Our last evening in Danang was spent in a very nice hotel and our guide showed up with a brand-new Honda 50 and I asked if I could try it out. He very generously let me ride it and I was off into the night. I found myself enveloped by the hugely crowded streets, filled with bikes just like the one I was riding. I couldn't slow down or stop in that flow of traffic, and I couldn't figure out where the light switch was – so I was running dark. Two young men on another Honda came alongside and one said, "you're not from here, are you?" and I said, "how could you tell?" He told me that the light switch was on the left grip, and I found it and turned the lights on.

He said, "we're heading for a party – would you like to come?" (all in perfect accentless American English). I told him that I couldn't – my wife was back at the hotel worrying about me and I needed to get back. The young guy said "welcome back!" and waved as I turned away. It was good to be back.

Appendix I

(Photo from the Author's Collection)

M422 Mighty Mite Jeep

The M422A1 Jeep was a Marine Corps-only vehicle that was ubiquitous in the early part of our involvement in Vietnam. It was tiny: only 9 1/2 feet long and 5 feet wide (For comparison, the 1965 VW Beetle was 13 feet long.) and made mostly of aluminum. We had it because when its specifications were written, the main helicopter we had was the Sikorsky UH-34 and that helicopter had trouble lifting itself on high altitude, hot days. So the Mighty Mite was tiny and light (it was so light that a reasonably strong man could lift the whole rear end of it up in the air). It was built by American Motors and had a V-4 air-cooled engine and since it was air cooled, it made a funny vacuum cleaner noise when it was running and it was surprisingly bullet-resistant since it didn't have a radiator. You could cram four large Marines into it – the two in front faced forward and the two in back sat on the sides with a folding back rest, facing each other – but it was so small that it looked like a large shoe skate with people sitting on top. It was pretty nimble and handled well and it had the astounding ability of balancing an open can of Coke on its transmission cover, just behind the gearshift so that it never spilled, even in a hard turn. Apparently that flat spot behind the gearshift is the exact position of the Center of Gravity. Some of the Mites mounted an M60 machine gun on a pedestal mount in the back and it was just high enough that you could shoot forward over the windshield if needed. As small as it was, and as rare as they turned out to be (and thus the parts are almost non-existent), the Mite was a very enjoyable ride and I would love to own one now.

M274 Mechanical Mule

The Mule was a strange and again as far as I know a Marine Corps-unique item that was really a large Go-Kart to be used to transport loads over short distances, though there was also a version that carried an awe-inspiring 106mm Recoilless Rifle. It was a flat-bed item with the driver's seat in front and it was powered by a flat four-cylinder air-cooled engine. It was started using a pull rope (!) and it had no body work at all – it was completely out in the open, except for a short rail around its perimeter. It had four fat little tires and no actual suspension so it could go cross-country but the ride would be back-breakingly rough. They were reasonably useful but difficult to maintain because the parts were scarce for some reason. I never got to drive one of those things, but I haven't lost any sleep over it.

M54 5-Ton Truck

This was my Alma Mater, the beast I learned to drive, more or less, at Camp Pendleton before I left for Vietnam. It was the early gas-fueled version and lacked all the extra plumbing and piping of the later multifuel versions of that truck. Like I said earlier, you could heat your C-Rations on the exhaust manifold by simply folding down the right side panel next to the hood. It was large and had two manual shifters: one with four forward gears and reverse and another for high range and low range gearing. An experienced and skilled operator could shift both levers at the same time, one arm through the steering wheel and achieve an astounding fluidity of acceleration with heavy loads. I never could do that. The 5-Ton was versatile and as I also said earlier, could carry 7 ½ tons of ammunition plus a trailer of more ammunition and still get down the road quickly but uncertainly as it tended to wander a lot with its front end up at an angle. Vietnam was hot, so we would open up the windshields (the two panes pivoted upward when you released the latches and then locked with a friction knob to hold them open) and there were vents by your feet that you could push open to let in more breeze. My M-14 fit nicely behind and to the left of my seat but it would have been hard to get to in a hurry if it was needed. Later on, we put sandbags on the floor of the cab to try to reduce the lethality of mines but that was certainly pointless: most 5-Tons and other vehicles that hit mines had the fronts almost completely torn off, so sandbags were more for morale than effect. The 5-Ton was versatile: there were cargo versions, wrecker versions, dump truck versions, fuel truck versions, and my personal favorite, the open water tanker version. It had an open top rubber bladder in the back that we would fill at the army water point near Phu Bai and when it was filled, you had to carefully and gingerly accelerate through the gears. Any small imperfection in acceleration/deceleration, any missed gears, any sudden braking and a massive wave of water would build up and pour over the top of the bladder forward into the open cab. Interesting combination of drowning and refreshing at the same time.

M35 2 ½ Ton Truck ("Deuce and a Half")

The Deuce and a Half was the workhorse of our war – they were everywhere, doing everything and in contrast to the 5-Ton, it was a joy to drive even though it didn't have power steering. Like the M54 5-Ton, our version was gas fueled and had the exhaust pipe exiting down and to the right, between the center and rear dual wheels. The reason I mention this is, that we realized early on that if you turned the ignition switch off while you were driving down the road, then waited a second or two and then turned it back on, the engine would backfire mightily, and a gout of flame would come out of the exhaust pipe and flamethrower anybody alongside you in that direction. Loads of fun, as long as you didn't do that to an MP or something. A very rugged and reasonably nimble truck and we used them to tow our M101A1 105mm howitzers.

Ontos escorting a convoy (Photo taken by Ramon R. Alba used with permission)

M50A1 "Ontos"

This is yet another Marine Corps-unique item and its nickname was "Sardine can with tracks." It was a small and lightly-armored vehicle with six 106mm recoilless rifles as its main armament and it was originally designed just at the end of the Korean War to kill tanks; thus it was assigned to Antitank battalions. It never got to do that: it was used for convoy security, point defense and as a kind of assault gun for infantry patrols. It was always funny to see that thing moving through tall grass, with an infantry Marine leading it on foot, and its two tall antennas waving above the grass like a big bug. It may have been funny-looking and flimsy (the 1 ½ inch armor couldn't stop much more than small arms and the bottom armor was even weaker – and since mines come through the bottom and the spare ammunition was stored in the floor, this was an important flaw) but in battle the damn thing was awe-inspiring. There were two .50 caliber "spotting rifles" on the upper two barrels that were ballistically matched to the 106mm rounds so when the spotting rounds were fired, they had tracers to show the path of the shot and when they hit; a puff of white phosphorus showed where they impacted. Once the gunner had everything pointed the right way, the Ontos could fire one round of 106mm, or two rounds together or ALL SIX at once, which was like your own personal End of the World. The 106mm recoilless rifle is "recoilless" because the same gas that was pushing its 35 pound warhead out of the barrel also exited the rear of the rifles as a sort of jet blast to balance things out. The noise and flash were stupefyingly loud and if you were self-destructive enough to stand behind it when it went off, they would be unable to find much left to bury. The blast effect of the 106mm round was huge too, much more than the comparable 105mm artillery round. The Ontos gunners were like snipers in that they almost always hit exactly where they needed to and an Ontos was an excellent fight-ender. There was one more flaw to its design: you had to get completely out of the Ontos to load the barrels. So much for armor protection!

As a funny postscript, I helped put together an Onto crewman's reunion at Quantico a few years ago, since we had the last known complete Ontos that had just been restored for the Marine Corps Museum.

About 50 former Ontos men and their families showed up and posed with our Ontos and some tried to get back into it but found that hard to do: they all marveled on how the "Ontos had shrunk" over time.

M48A1 90mm Tank

This metal monster was a mainstay for guarding critical bridges and sometimes escorting convoys or patrols but the terrain severely limited their employment cross-country. During the later Battle of Hue City, they were critical to the offensive operations by providing protection to the troops using them as cover and for their ability to face storms of small arms fire while very effectively taking out barricaded NVA troops. They were also used to evacuate the wounded.

The narrow roads on Vietnam barely allowed them to fit and opposing direction traffic had to find a wider spot in the road to get out of the way while they passed. One of the striking things about that tank was how quiet it was: if it was moving slowly forward, you could feel the beat of the engine in your chest but could barely hear it as it crept along. The weaponry included its 90mm cannon which fired a high explosive projectile and also a canister round that was like a large shotgun. It also had at least one .50 caliber machine gun and a coaxial .30 caliber machine gun. There was a telephone in a box at the rear of the tank that allowed you to speak to the tank commander and direct him to a target.

If you could get the tank out to where you were, they were very effective weapons. The problem was getting them out there. We had one tank sink up to its fenders in the mud in front of our artillery position and couldn't get itself out. They sent a huge, powerful tank retriever out to get that tank and as we watched, the towing cable glowed red and then snapped with a loud bang and the end of the broken cable tore the machine gun and mount completely off the retriever. After that, they left it there and when I went back to Vietnam in 2000, it was still there.

An M-53 155mm Self-propelled howitzer. (Photo by Ramon R. Alba, used with permission)

M53/M54 Self-Propelled Howitzer.

These were the heavy artillery that we had in the beginning years and they were large and ungainly but provided that heavy punch that you sometimes needed. They were essentially the same weapons except one, the M53, was in 155mm and the other, the M54 was in 8 inch (203mm) caliber. Both of them were based on an old tank chassis, had gasoline engines and if the driver was in a humorous mood, he could make them backfire a huge gout of flames out of its left side to flame unsuspecting people. Huge fun if you were riding in the back of truck when they did that. My other memory of the 8-inch version was the time I decided to nap on the sandbag wall in front of our gun position. While I was sleeping, the 8-inch gun was rolled into that position and I woke just as the damn thing fired, throwing me into the air and enveloping me in its considerable blast. It was a while before I could hear anything at all.

M50 "Howtar" (Photo from the Author's collection)

M50 Howtar 4.2 Inch ("Four Deuce") Mortar

This little and freakish weapon was another attempt to get around the inade-quacies of our early helicopter lift by installing a 4.2 inch (107mm) mortar tube on an old 75mm Pack Howitzer carriage, hence the name "Howtar"

(Howitzer and Mortar, get it?). The mortar was originally a chemical (as in poison gas) weapon, but it turned out to more useful delivering high explosive rounds in its original WWII and Korean War form. It was a rifled mortar, so it was somewhat more accurate than a smoothbore mortar. On its Pack Howitzer carriage, it couldn't elevate high enough to achieve its high-angle capabilities, so Howtars were usually emplaced with their wheels mounted on a stack of sand-filled wooden ammunition boxes to elevate them sufficiently to fire them.

The batteries of them – one per artillery battalion – were called "Whiskey" Batteries.

Unfortunately for us, they proved to be less than optimum fire support. Sometimes the tubes would get water in them (it did rain in Vietnam) or the propellant increments were old (they looked like slices of old cheese) and the mortar would shoot "short" or fly erratically which wasn't at all entertaining if you were in front of them. I was bracketed by a Whiskey battery early in my time as a forward observer and I was lucky not to be killed. The grim joke among us forward observers was "what is your next command if the Message to Observer includes the word "Whiskey?" Answer: send "End of mission."

M29 81mm Mortar ("Piss Tube")
This was the standard company mortar for us and was carried by Marines from battalion Weapons Company in three more-or-less portable parts: the barrel ("tube") about 100 pounds altogether, sight, tube, bipod and the baseplate. Most of the rest of us in the infantry company carried three rounds for it on a backpack frame, which added 60 pounds to our already crazy load of nearly a hundred pounds of helmet, flak jacket, cartridge belt with loaded magazines, weapon and water and food. Did I mention that it was always hot? Nonetheless, a very effective, deadly weapon that fired a scary-good High Explosive round, plus white phosphorus, and illumination rounds. Probably worth the suffering caused by carrying it around.

M101A1 Howitzer (Photo by Ramon R. Alba, used with permission)

M101A1 105mm Howitzer

The "One-Oh-Five" was the main artillery weapon of our war. The Marine Corps had the M101 throughout the war but the army picked up the M102 lightweight 105mm early in the war which was a very different weapon that could turn in a full circle, using a small fat tire at the rear that was cranked to aim the weapon. Our M101 was a conventional and heavy WWII-era weapon that could reach out to 11,000 meters, firing a 33-pound High Explosive projectile. You could crank it up high in the air to fire like a mortar, or fire it at low angles to attack targets directly. You could with some skill (and a corresponding lack of caution) fire it ten or more times a minute and it was reasonably (for 1966) accurate. It weighed 5,600 pounds and if you weren't well-muscled before you landed on its gun section, you sure were afterward. We fired High Explosive, White Phosphorus ("Willie Pete"), Illumination, and Smoke projectiles from those beasts as I say in my story, sometimes almost a thousand in a day. You spent any non-firing moments of those days cleaning it and since it is the Marine Corps, repainting it so it looked picture-perfect. Weird. One of my first chores on the 105 was to clean the breechblock. Nothing to it: the forward right-hand side had a release pin and once that was removed, the 90-pound block slid easily out the side for cleaning. We used oil and emery cloth to shine that puppy up and when all of its parts were reassembled and ready, you slid that beast back in – except that I forgot to put that pin back in and the newly shiny and oily block slid right through to the other side and fell in the sand! Had to take it completely apart and reclean it from scratch.

LVTH-6

This was an attempt by the Marine Corps to combine good healthy fire support to an amphibious assault by combining an amphibious tractor with a 105mm howitzer in an armored turret. In Vietnam, these somewhat uncommon vehicles were used as supplementary fire support, usually attached to an artillery battalion and farmed out as needed for additional mass. They were referred to as "How-6s" and their callsign on the radio was "Combine" as in "Combine Bravo," etc. They were huge slab-sided beasts and like the amphibian they were based on, the gas tanks were in the floor and you had the same fun of a massive fire if it hit a mine with the added element of the stored howitzer ammunition on board. They were not very successful in the fire support role in my experience. Either their indirect fire training or procedures were inadequate or the flexing of the suspension of the vehicle during recoil threw things off or both, but they had the reputation of being inaccurate and occasionally dangerous to us instead of the enemy. Like the Howtar "Whiskey" batteries, you stood a better than average chance of shelling yourself if you called for a fire mission that included the "Combine" battery and it was another time the correct answer would be "end of mission."

M114 155mm Howitzer being fired in Hawaii. (Photo from Author's Collection)

M114A1 Howitzer ("the Pig")

I think that I covered the "Pig" fairly well in my story, but I should probably mention that as large and heavy as it was, the later versions of the 155mm howitzer were even larger and heavier – 7.5 tons for the M198! But since we're talking about the Vietnam War, the Pig was the biggest towed cannon system I had to deal with. One of the signature features of the Pig was its shiny gun tube – which actually formed part of its unique annular recoil system – and it had to be kept shiny and oily to function. We used a rope wrapped once around the gun tube and some oily solvent, pulled back and forth between teams of us to keep it clean and polished.

3.5 Inch Rocket Launcher

The 3.5 was developed during Korea to deal with the thick-hided Soviet tanks and it was called the "Super Bazooka." It was a large, fat and long tube to fire a fairly large rocket and it had a front grip with the trigger, a steel strap shoulder rest and a small optical sight on the left side. It had several different kinds of rocket that you could use, including High Explosive Antitank (HEAT) and White Phosphorus. It was more or less accurate but required two operators: one to aim and one to load. The Loader would remove the safety band from the rocket and insert in into the back of the launcher and then press a lever down, which connected the electrical connection to the rocket. The Gunner would aim at the target and the trigger was a mushy-feeling electrical generator that ignited the rocket motor. Like the LAW, the noise it made in firing was a loud bang and the rocket completely used up its motor impulse within the length of the launcher tube. Also like the LAW, nobody that you liked should be behind that thing when it fired. Because of its backblast, firing it while within an enclosed space was a really bad idea. The ballistics of that thing were a bit of an arc, so a Gunner really had to be well-skilled to actually hit anything at extended range. The tube easily broke down into two halves, which made carrying it less arduous; however, the rockets were heavy and bulky, and they were spread out among everyone to share the load. I think that it was considered an antique even when we had it.

The M26 Frag Grenade

Hand grenades are simple, intimate weapons. They are cool to the touch when you remove them from their cardboard tube container and the safety ring jingles slightly when you pick it up. The oval, smooth shape of the M26s we carried in Vietnam fit perfectly on the palm of the hand. Its olive green skin was sheet steel covering a few ounces of square steel wire, notched to fragment better, wrapped around a charge of about 6 ounces of Composition B. It weighed just about one pound even and a guy in average shape can throw the thing almost 100 feet. Through some hours of training and then later experience you knew that bending the ends of the cotter pin attached to the safety ring eased its removal but not to bend it too straight, since you never wanted it to fall out. Once the grenade was firmly in the palm of your hand, safety lever (the "spoon") held in the web between your thumb and forefinger, that ring was what you used to ready the whole four and one half second train of events the M26 was born to do. Once the ring and its pin came out of its hole, the spoon was free to open and flip away from the grenade body and a fuze ignited. Almost exactly 4 ½ seconds later, the filler would detonate no matter where it was at that moment – in your pouch, or at your feet, or rolling next to the enemy where you intended. It took guts to hold that thing for a second or two more after you intentionally released the spoon – while you knew that that fuze was hissing quietly away inside it – to make sure that the grenade would go off near the enemy instead of possibly getting that murderous thing thrown right back to you.

At the instant it did go off, those notched sections of steel wire expanded and broke apart into hundreds of sharp white-hot pieces, expanding away from the center at speeds ten times faster than a rifle bullet. By the book, the M26 had a casualty radius of 15 meters from the center of that detonation but more often those speeding fragments carried deadly effects much farther and it was obvious to all of us who used this smooth-skinned little killer that no one could possibly throw one far enough to escape unharmed on open ground. Nearly every infantryman I knew in Vietnam had one or more steel bits from their own grenades in them. You would try to get some cover when you threw them, but it wasn't always possible. It was just part of the nastiness that was our world and you accepted that. I would carry four of them on average, four extra pounds to add to the water, ammunition, body armor and rifle but they were irreplaceable when the enemy was close—somewhere just on the other side of a green wall of vegetation. Grenades are the close-in weapon of desperation, when your enemy is almost close enough to touch and you are willing to injure yourself in the process of stopping him. Grenades were the all-purpose tool for entering caves and bunkers to make sure nobody living was waiting for you when you had to go in. Grenades were the weapon you used at night when you could hear the enemy crawling, scraping in the grass near you in the darkness and you couldn't risk the muzzle flash of your rifle or machine gun showing everyone where you were. Our M26s often ended up in the enemy's hands and they would craft them into vicious traps. They would shorten the fuze inside to go off instantaneously when the spoon was released, then shorten the spoon until it was just a short nub and then place it into a C-ration can that had been nailed to the base of a small tree, about a foot or two off the ground. They would string a thin wire across the trail, down in the grass where it was invisible and attach it to the top of the grenade and it would wait there for one of us to lightly drag a toe into the wire. Those things almost always tore the legs off the poor guy that tripped it and ripped into all of the men up and down the trail from him. One second everyone's fine, the next second a whole squad is lying on the ground, parts irrevocably torn from their bodies, blood pouring, lives extinguished.

In the movies, grenades make a familiar "boom" sound usually accompanied by a fountain of flame. The movie special effects people have made that version so familiar that anyone who actually hears a real grenade go off is surprised when they hear that distinctive sound. Grenades don't make a simple "boom" sound: It's a sharp, deep crack, a metallic punch with an accompanying whistle of the fragments flying. Like a huge steel door slamming fast. It's short and sharp and only a small grey cloud of smoke and dust is visible. The real sound raises the hair on the back of your neck, and you can hear it for years afterward, in the edge of your mind. People who have not seen combat sometimes snicker when they see some guy contort his body into a curl and crouch downward when there is an unexpected loud noise like maybe fireworks. That reaction stays with you for the rest of your life when your mind and body remember the shock and pain of those damned pieces hitting you and those around you.

US Rifle, Semiautomatic, M-14 outfitted as I carried it while I was assigned to the infantry. The bipod is the early XM-3 "clothespin" M-16 bipod clipped onto the gas cylinder and the sling is attached to the wrist of the stock at the rear and in the front, attached to a Blanket Roll Strap that attaches to the barrel above the gas cylinder. This arrangement allowed me to carry it on my right shoulder, pointing forward at waist height and very quickly employed right or left to respond to ambushes. Another fine example of enlisted ingenuity.

M-14 Rifle

When we started out in Vietnam, the M-14 was our standard rifle for everybody. It was in 7.62mm NATO caliber, but it was essentially an M-1 Garand rifle in a new caliber, with a much better gas system and a 20-round magazine.

It was the last of the old-fashioned "wood and steel" weapons and though heavy in comparison with today's rifles, it was easy enough to get used to and fire well. Unlike the M-16, it had excellent sights that were readily adjustable for different ranges, different conditions and a skilled rifleman could easily hit a man out to 500m if you had a nice, solid firing position. Most of them as issued had a Selector Lock which limited them to semiautomatic fire only but a small, easily obtained kit would replace the Selector lock with a Selector and you were in the full-auto business once it was installed. The Selector was at the right rear of the receiver and rotating the pointed end upward gave you full-auto fire – and this could be done in the dark quite easily by feel. In full-auto the M-14 was quite difficult to control if you didn't have a lot of practice and/or a bipod: it had a rate of fire around 800 rounds per minute and you could empty the 20-round magazine in a single trigger pull. But when you had the trigger control down, it was dead simple to put rounds exactly where you wanted them. Best of all the M-14 was supremely dependable and always, always fired when you needed it to and you hit somebody with it, they went down and stayed there.

It came with a reasonably short and sturdy bayonet but I never had any occasion to use it on anyone. All of my leaders were nice, rational guys and never considered conducting WWI-style bayonet charges. It was useful for breaking the steel straps that banded ammunition boxes or the wires around C-Ration boxes.

After I got back from Vietnam and the hospital, I was talking to one of my high school buddies, Bob D, who had served with the Army 82nd Airborne Division in Vietnam and our conversation devolved into arguing about the M-16/M-14 controversy. He told me that the "M-14 was too long and too heavy for Vietnam, but the M-16 was much better because it was lighter, and you could carry more ammunition." I told him that I wished that he told me – so I could have sent him a "big, strong Marine to hold the weapon up for him". He doesn't talk to me much anymore.

During the Iraq War, a friend of mine was commanding an artillery battalion as a "provisional infantry battalion" in al Anbar province and they were having difficulty engaging the enemy at the long distances they often encountered or firing through the walls the enemy frequently hid behind. The latest versions of the M-16 weren't up to the job, so he asked me to see if I could get some M-14 rifles for his men. There wasn't any question that the M-14 is an excellent long-distance rifle and could punch through any wall in Iraq – so he had the right man to get them to him. At that time, I was working for the Marine Corps Warfighting Lab at Quantico, so I had the connections that he needed. I found over 2,000 good, serviceable condition M-14s in storage and then located the slings, ammunition, magazines, magazine pouches, repair parts and armorer's tools and gauges and got ready to send them in theater when Headquarters Marine Corps got wind of it and ordered me to cancel everything. Their reasoning was that the "new Designated Marksman's Rifle (DMR) would be in service soon"; so getting those M-14s to the troops in Iraq was unnecessary. The result was my friend's battalion never got any new weapons and I'm fairly sure the DMR program has disappeared too. Things never change.

M76 Grenade Launcher and Grenade Adapter with dummy M-26 grenade installed

The M76 was a simple steel tube with a small locking mechanism at one end that allowed you to turn your M-14 into a grenade launcher – and what a launcher! You could fire real M26 grenades, not those little wimpy 40mm Blooper grenades but a one pound nightmare M26 with real punch. The Grenade Adapter fit over the end of that tube once it was mounted on the muzzle of your M14 and it was a simple steel tube with a tail fin assembly to stabilize it and a bracket for holding the grenade. There were a couple of drawbacks to this lashup: the M-14 needed a special crimped blank cartridge loaded into it to propel the heavy grenade and adapter the 100 meters or so it could go and the gas valve for the M-14 had to be switched off to prevent wrecking the gas system with the massive pressure. Also, it had bone-breaking recoil when it was fired, so you had to rest the rifle butt on the ground. Nonetheless, some of us would set everything up as we left the position, heavy grenade on the front of our rifle and when we cleared the barbed wire; we would pull the pin on the grenade, since the adapter held the safety lever in place. The instant we were in contact, you'd aim the rifle like a mortar towards the enemy and if you got the angle right, the M26 grenade would arc through the air and detonate right in the middle of the enemy. If you did that right, fight over. You had to remember to switch the gas system back on afterward or you were stuck with a manually-operated bolt-action rifle.

SSgt D was an artist with that thing, and he always seemed to get that grenade exactly where we needed it.

M1911A1 .45 caliber Pistol

The .45 was the same beast as developed for WWI and then modified for use in WWII and Korea and it was another quality weapon from a bygone era where they actually spent good money to arm us. It was completely dependable, and it killed immediately, first shot. As you probably read in my story, I owe my life to the one-shot lethality of this world-class pistol (aimed by a dog). It is, once again, a John Moses Browning design; so it didn't require pampering to work. One of our radio operators carried a .45 in a shoulder holster and just let it rust, since he had decided that he'd "go through the whole war without firing a shot" for whatever reason goofy kids do things. Then, as he was following our Company Commander down a trail through a village, a VC with an extended bayonet on his rifle came out of a doorway behind the captain and our radio operator drew his .45 and killed the VC with one shot. The slide had locked back, thanks to the radio operator's neglect but when it was needed; it worked quite well.

M-16 Rifle ("Mouse Gun," "Matty Mattel")

We started to get the first M-16s in late '66 and early '67 and as I mention in the story, they had a high failure rate. The M-16 was undeniably light and you could carry hundreds of rounds of ammunition but since it could seize up at any time and become unfirable; it wasn't a great asset to have the first couple of years that we had it. As I stated in the story, the jams were horrific: the extractor tore the base of the fired cartridge off and then a live cartridge was fed into the stuck remainder of the previous cartridge and the whole thing locked up the chamber and the bolt into an unclearable mess. Your only option was to take the thing partially apart and try to knock the jam out, using an assembled cleaning rod (some of the guys carried those cleaning rods for ready use by drilling a hole into the rear of the M16 plastic handguard and using it like a 19th Century muzzle loader's ramrod).

Several investigating teams came to Vietnam to allegedly find out the causes of this disaster, but they all seemed to "circle the wagons" and blame us for "not cleaning them well enough." We did clean them very well – I watched everyone around me cleaning them daily – but good cleaning had no effect at all. The truth was that the ammunition we were provided used a different powder than that which they had used for testing and the new powder formed a type of glue in the chamber that guaranteed jamming. I wrote to Congress, telling my congressman that our rifles were defective and that: "I don't care if you have to gold plate the interior of our weapons and use sapphire bearings, we need the best available weapons to keep us alive." I didn't receive a response. As also mentioned earlier, its "devastating" ammunition most often wasn't, and men visibly hit often kept running. It did fire full-auto and was very controllable in that mode but that engendered the "spray and pray" method of fire that only infrequently connected with anyone you meant to hit. As I said earlier, the sights were a screwable front post that were meant to be adjusted by a bullet tip (as were the rear sights) and the adjustments were hard to track, since there was no way to accurately measure count the revolutions of that screw. The end result was that the M-16 could be roughly adjusted, if you had the time and freedom to do so, to hit reasonably well at a certain range but firing at nearer or farther ranges required guessing where the round would hit and often that guess gave you a miss. Beside the self-fouling gas system and the inaccessible chamber, the early M-16's safety would jam on "Safe" and releasing the safety required hitting it with something hard, like the back of a bayonet, to make it ready to fire. The early magazines were substandard too and the allegedly 20 round magazine could only hold 18 rounds if you wanted it to work at all. As I said in my story, I kept my M-14 the whole damn time I was in Vietnam because it always worked when you needed it to work. The people who pushed for the M-16 to be fielded before it was properly tested in the operational environment should be held responsible for hundreds of deaths of our own guys and the loss their families will always carry with them when that unfinished weapon failed them when they needed it most.

M79 Grenade Launcher ("Blooper")

Its nickname came from the muffled "pop" it made when you fired it and it operated on an unusual "high-low" pressure system where a small amount of propellant detonated in an open space behind the fat projectile, and it was accelerated down its rifled bore at relatively low pressure. The M79 40mm grenade launcher was an interesting weapon: it was essentially a small mortar with a tilted-up rifle stock that opened like a single-barrel shotgun. It had a folding ladder sight which seemed to be more or less precise, but it had three important issues:

1. It required the firer to expose his head and shoulders above cover to aim and fire it.
2. The fired round had a steep "rainbow" trajectory and a long time of flight, which meant that you had to stay exposed to enemy fire to watch where it eventually hit and make any corrections.
3. The round itself wasn't tremendously powerful. It had a small spherical grenade in the middle of the round plus a complex bore safety system. That left little room within that small grenade for much in the way of high explosives and the fragments – the lethal part – were tiny. You had to virtually hit the individual you were aiming at to actually kill him – and hitting anything required a lot of practice and skill. I used that thing exactly once in combat and discovered how many shots it took to get close to the intended target and how exposed I was while I did it. It is very unlikely I did anything that day except add to the noise levels. But a more skilled Blooper gunner was a sight to behold! They could hit a running man at long distance through their almost preternatural ability to calculate where to aim to allow for the trajectory, the time of flight and the place that guy would be when the round arrived.

M-60 Machine Gun

The M-60 machine gun was almost an icon of the Vietnam War: it was reasonably light, had a steady rate of fire and when it was running properly, kept a stream of 7.62 mm NATO exactly where you wanted it out to 600m and further. It was, however a "least bidder" weapon made nice and inexpensively from stampings, castings, pop rivets and plastic. While it worked most of the time, it regularly chipped bolts, broke firing pins, and even melted barrels. (Oddly, the German MG-42 from WWII was also a cheaply made weapon but it was engineered far better and – unfortunately for us – supremely dependable.) When the grunts went through our artillery battery, they routinely stole parts from our machine guns to keep theirs running. It was annoying but understandable, since the machine gun is the foundation of infantry offensive and defensive firepower, and our supply system was terrible. One would think that the Powers That Be in the Pentagon would have realized how critical – how essential to life itself – dependable weapons were to us. But in the end, cost won out. Only decades later were the M-60s replaced with a more expensive but far more dependable machine gun. I used the M-60 many times and I was fortunate that it did always function for me, but I had a very pampered gun and never had to deal with extended and desperate bursts where my life depended on it outlasting the enemy.

**Note the telescopic sight bracket on this one at the right rear of the receiver.
(Photo by Ramon R. Alba, used with permission)**

M-2 .50 caliber Machine Gun

As you saw in my story, it was a while before I mastered the setup and use of this magnificent heavy machine gun. But once I did, it was absolutely dependable and devastating against any and all targets. It was heavy: when I was newbie in Vietnam, a Staff NCO told be to carry the M2 to the top of a short hill. The whole machine gun with tripod weighed over 120 pounds and because I was a newbie – and obedient – I carried that whole gun and tripod on my shoulders to the top and my legs felt like rubber when I got there. The older salts all laughed at me, since anyone with more than a few minutes of training would know that the M2 disassembles easily into three loads – the barrel, the receiver and of course, the tripod. The M2 could and did hit point targets out to a mile and some of the older ones even had a bracket for a sniper scope. Once that gun's tripod was firmly seated and the weapon was locked to a Traversing and Elevation (T&E) mechanism (a kind of micrometer adjustment system that could accurately hold the gun firmly and allow exact left-right and up-down movement) that gun could pick out a single man-sized target out to a mile and farther. It had a voice all of its own; a steady full-throated boom and steady rhythm. The bullet itself for that gun was huge and could punch through light armor, sandbag walls, houses, concrete – you name it. It was after, all a design from the greatest firearms designer of all time – John Moses Browning – and it worked forever. It dated to a time when only the best was produced for our soldiers, cost be damned.

M-3A1 "Greasegun" submachinegun

At the other end of the cost line was the very inexpensive and heavy M3A1 "Greasegun." It was originally produced in WWII as a lower-cost replacement to the M1 Thompson submachinegun and it was designed to fire the same .45 caliber pistol round. It was as simple a device as could be, relying on the inertia of a large, heavy bolt to hold the cartridge in place while the bullet left the barrel. You cocked the bolt by sticking a finger (!) in a hole in the bolt to pull it back and ready it for firing. The "safety" was a folding door dust cover that held the bolt in place while it was closed. It had a very slow rate of fire and a lot of recoil, and it took a lot of practice to really control it and while you could do single shots with good trigger control, it was sort of pointless as that big bolt slid forward hard and disturbed any aim you had going for you. Its maximum effective range was about 50-70 yards and when you did the "Steve McQueen" and taped two 30-round magazines end-to-end, it weighed more than my M-14 fully loaded. Since my M-14 was infinitely more effective and could nail the enemy out to where he was, I got rid of the Greasegun and went back to the '14.

LAW 66mm Rocket Launcher

Even though we almost never saw enemy tanks in Vietnam, the Light Antitank Weapon (LAW) was a much-appreciated item in our arsenal. It was a compact, disposable rocket launcher that weighed only a few pounds and it was easy to carry two or three of them on their slings as part of your combat load. They were used as a kind of "portable artillery" and they were accurate to about 200m with practice and about perfect for taking out machine guns or bunkers. When you were going to fire one, you pulled the pin at the rear of it which released the carrying sling and end caps, allowing you to pull it open, extending its length and causing the two sights to pop out into position. You placed it on your shoulder, pulled a safety forward ahead of the rear sight and when you had it lined up, you squeezed the rubber "tit" trigger just in front of the rear sight. It would go off with a loud bang and if your eye was quick enough, you'd see a black streak of the rocket flying towards the target. It's funny, but movies that try to feature the LAW always show it slowly leaving the tube with a "whoosh" with a lot of smoke. Ridiculous. It was lightning- fast and the motor completely burned itself out before it even left the tube, making a loud bang when it went off. The explosion it made on the target was large and satisfying and usually all you needed to nail an enemy firing position. There was a funny incident when I was out with the grunts where one of the guys fired a LAW during a very heavy firefight where the enemy was about 300m away. He readied his LAW and then boldly went into the open, knelt on one knee, and aimed his LAW upward about 45 degrees to try to extend its range to the enemy tree line. He fired and the backblast from his LAW flipped him into the air and he spun, spread-eagled, three full revolutions before he landed flat on his face in the field. All the firing stopped, and everybody was laughing – even the enemy (we could hear them laughing) – and nobody fired for a few seconds. The Marine got up and shook himself and ran back to cover and as the fight resumed, and his rocket hit pretty well where he wanted it to.

Claymore Mine

A nasty little beauty from our war, it was about 10 inches across and 6 inches high and made of green plastic and had little metal folding feet to prop it up. It was curved and the convex surface, helpfully labelled—"This side towards Enemy"—was propped up on the ground and a blasting cap was inserted into a fuze well in the top, with wires extending some distance away. The mine was filled with stacked ball bearings in two rows and an explosive layer behind it. When the bad guys showed, you'd squeezed the hand generator ("Hell Box") and Pow! that little charmer mowed them down.

Appendix 2

VIETCONG AND NVA UNIFORMS

THE VIETCONG DIDN'T HAVE MANY "STANDARDIZED" UNIFORMS but wore the same kinds of clothing as the general populace: loose, cotton billowy trousers and shirts with two chest pockets in black and sometimes white material, though they also had green uniforms as well. They wore sandals made of auto tires ("Ho Chi Minh Sandals") and had round crowned hats with an all-around short brim that was effective at keeping the rain and sun off and helped blend their shape into their background. The main things that distinguished them from the civilians around them were their cartridge belts and chest harness for carrying their rifle magazines or stripper clips for their rifles and their distinctive haircuts. The VC had longish hair on top, rapidly tapering towards the bottom and even when they had ditched their weapons and equipment, made them instantly recognizable as VC anyway.

The North Vietnamese Army had green uniforms, often with colored cloth patches on their upper sleeves for identification and wore their distinctive "Hard Hat" pith helmets. They were well outfitted with combat gear, with excellent packs and cartridge/magazine carriers to support their modern weapons. Their stuff was light and well suited for the climate and the long distances they had to march. A prized souvenir were their belts – they had a green cotton belt with an aluminum buckle with a red star at the center that was simple and well made – so we usually grabbed those things as soon as the shooting had stopped, and the previous owner was done with it.

ENEMY WEAPONS AND EQUIPMENT

Stick Grenade

The enemy had several versions of these grenades, but most of them had a fragmenting segmented head made of cast iron or simple sheet steel head and contained a few ounces of explosive with a short, usually bamboo, handle. The whole grenade was about 7-9 inches long altogether and had a groove around the wood handle to grip it while it was being flung. There was a cork at the bottom of the handle attached to a cord within the handle and as you got ready to use it, you'd pull the cork and its attached string, which would ignite the fuse train and you'd throw it. They were a sort of "light switch" weapon: you'd either be hit when it went off or you wouldn't. The fragmentation was pretty random, so there was a fair chance the damn thing would just rattle you when it went off. Or not. We were not inclined to use them when we captured them because they had two versions of fuse: 4 seconds or zero seconds, for use as a booby trap. Since none of us knew which was which, we didn't try them out when we had them.

In 1977, when I was assigned to Okinawa, I found one of these grenades in the upper drawer of my office desk. The Warrant Officer who had that desk before told me: "not to worry – it's inert." I eased the cork out slightly and saw that it was still attached to its cord and called the base Explosive Ordnance Disposal and they found that it was, after all those years, still quite alive.

M44 Moisin-Nagant Rifle/Chinese Type 53

A short bolt-action WWII Russian-designed rifle with a built-in long spike bayonet that you could pivot in place quickly. It was in a powerful 7.62mm caliber and vastly outclassed by everything we had but there were a lot of them, and they were rugged and dependable. Best of all, they qualified as a legal war souvenir and if you captured one, you could bring it home with you.

SKS Carbine

Another Russian-designed weapon that fired the shorter and more modern 7.62 X 39 caliber semiautomatically from a built-in 10 round magazine. It also had a built-in bayonet but the VC almost always removed the bayonet to save weight and probably any temptation to get close enough to us to use it. I had a captured SKS that was my favorite souvenir, and I would get ammo from the grunts to shoot it. One day in the battery, we had a sniper fire at us with what had to be an SKS with its distinctive "Poit" sound and firing a green tracer. Coincidentally, my SKS was filled with green tracers and I used it to shoot back at the sniper. There was a long pause, and then the sniper shot again, his green tracer zipping through our position and I shot back with my green tracer. Another longer pause and the sniper shot again, and I shot back. The sniper quit at that point – apparently convinced that all of his shots were bouncing back to him! You could, with proper authorization, bring an SKS home too but my SKS was stolen by Captain R, the Battalion S-2, on the pretense that it was a "rare intelligence item" and I later found that he had in turn sold it to another officer. The SKS has a short stock which doesn't fit most average-size Americans and its open rear sight doesn't lend itself to precision aiming, but it's handy size and light weight make it easy to carry and its silent safety makes it stealthy for night ambushes. It was another legal favorite to capture and bring home – as long as no one on your chain of command stole it first.

DP Machine gun
As I mentioned in the story, it had a long conical flash hider at the end of its barrel and a disc-shaped magazine on top which made it instantly recognizable. It had a steady rate of fire and seemed to be accurate, but it was older and ob-solete compared to the better machine guns the NVA had. Old or not, it wasn't something you approached with any enthusiasm.

Goryunov Machine Gun
Another heavier and older Russian-designed weapon but with a short piece of armor shield and small spoked wheels. Used the larger and older 7.62 X 54 rimmed cartridge and had a steady, somewhat fast rate of fire (well, anything shot faster than our M-60s). Way too heavy and cumbersome for Vietnam but once in place, very dependable and could shoot very steadily for a while with its belt feeding system. I'll bet the VC hated carrying that thing though.

K-50 Submachinegun
A custom NVA version of the Russian PPsH-41 submachinegun with a tall front sight, and truncated barrel jacket, and a French-style sliding wire stock. Shot very fast, about a rate of one thousand rounds per minute and with a 35-

round magazine, it emptied quickly. The magazines were difficult to load in a hurry so what you had loaded was all you had in a firefight. We captured one when the round in the chamber failed to go off and that small hesitation was the end of its owner. I still have that round with the dent in its primer. We fired that thing a lot in our battery position – like I said earlier, the VC had "donated" 25,000 rounds of pistol ammunition, left in one of our bunkers while we were away. We noticed two things: the bullets were hitting sideways when we fired it into the sand – the bore was nearly gone and the empty cartridge cases hit the ground about a foot above where the bullets hit, propelled by the bolt in a trajectory that matched the aim of the weapon! When my wife and I were visiting Danang in 2000, we went to their museum and I spotted a K-50 in a bundle of other weapons in an open display. I looked around for our guide or somebody from the museum to give me permission to handle it – but there wasn't anyone around, so I picked it up and showed it to my wife. I was taking it apart for her when a horrified guard showed up and made me put it back.

AMERICAN-MADE WEAPONS

The enemy made wide use of the weapons they captured or stole from us and our allies and apparently, the Chinese also had big stocks of US-made weapons to draw from and they were shipped south to the Vietcong. They had M16s, M1 rifles and carbines, Thompson submachineguns and Browning .30 caliber machine guns. We generally assumed the enemy had taken them from our dead, so we were usually less than forgiving when we found them on them.

NORTH VIETNAMESE ARMY WEAPONS AND EQUIPMENT

AK-47
The standard NVA issued rifle that was modern, effective and very reliable. It was prized item to capture but not to use: it made a very distinctive champagne-cork "pop" that would immediately draw fire from your nearest neighbors as soon as you pulled the trigger. The lucky thing for us was that the enemy almost always had the thing set for full-auto (the first safety position) and once they

fired it, if the first round didn't hit you, the rest would sail over your head. The recoil was enough to push the rifle upward and away from you. According to Lt. G, he and my Radio Operator Cpl. R spotted two VC parallel to the trail they were on and the two of them raced after them. As they turned a corner, with the larger Cpl. R in the lead, they stopped virtually face-to-face with the VC, who had turned around and were aiming their AKs at the Marines chasing them. The nearest VC fired, and Cpl. R flew across the trail and lay on his back, eyes closed. Lt. G. Fired at the enemy, apparently hitting no one and they escaped. Lt. G ran to Cpl. R and leaning over him said: "are you hit?"

Cpl. R opened one eye and said—"are they gone yet?" They missed him completely.

It also had somewhat simple sights and a short barrel, so long-distance hits were rare. The rate of fire of that rifle was a main feature of the bedlam of firefights, with hundreds, even thousands of rounds all fired at once. Unlike our M16, the AK-47 was stovebolt reliable and would continue to work even when filled with mud, rust, and other debris. Far better suited to Vietnam's climate than the unfortunate M-16. Many other countries adopted the AK platform and even some allied or neutral countries built their own versions (Israel, Finland, Switzerland, South Africa, and many others) and found them reliable. Once again, our government avoided any chance of building a more reliable combat weapon built on the good characteristics of the AK and just hung on the flawed AR-15/M-16 design.

RPD Machine gun
A long-barreled, bipod-equipped weapon with a large drum magazine, firing the same type of ammunition as the AK-47. Dangerous, effective, dependable. Likely what was used to shoot me.

RPK Machine gun
A magazine-fed machine gun also based on the AK-47 but a longer barrel fitted with a bipod. Rugged, dependable, dangerous. A very good machinegun.

120mm Mortar
A Russian or Chinese made mortar based on the design the Russians stole from the French Brandt mortar. Range of about 7,000 meters and very powerful and effective. Not enormously accurate and hard to carry around but when they used them, it was awe-inspiring.

122mm Rocket
A long and effective ballistic rocket system that was sometimes fired from improvised launchers by the VC. Flew about 16 Km and had "to whom it may concern" accuracy, but when your target was a large airfield or base, they couldn't miss. Very effective point-detonating fuze and HE fragmentary warhead.

B-40 (RPG-2) Rocket
A simple and early version of the RPG (Ruchnoy Protivotankivoy Grenato-mat–"Infantry antitank Grenade Launcher"), with a shaped charge armor-defeating warhead. Pure death for armored vehicles and very little fun for infantry when they fired them at us. The rocket loaded from the front, you cocked the hammer, you aimed it using its rough open sights, and Bang! The expelling charge would send it forward and then the fins opened at the rear when it came out of the tube and then the main rocket motor ignited, accelerating at you. Very nasty, with a large, effective warhead. Never understood why we didn't copy that thing for ourselves.

122mm and 152mm Howitzers
The NVA had some artillery that they brought south but most of it stayed in the vicinity of their strongholds, like the A Shau valley or the DMZ. Their guns were Russian-made, simple and powerful. We had a 122 in our neighborhood south of Danang once and it was quite the experience. Our company was taking a break during a patrol to eat lunch and play some cards when we heard a loud bang out in the open a couple of hundred meters away. Everybody glared at me, since it was clearly artillery, and I was the artillery observer. The company commander told me to "cancel all H&Is; so I called the battery on the radio. "Cancel all Hotel Indias in this area." There was a long pause and then another louder bang closer to us, this time clearly in view in the middle of an open rice paddy.

Then my battery got back to us and said, "There are no Hotel Indias in effect in your area". Then as we were absorbing that bit of information, another much louder bang even closer than the last time.

"That's enemy artillery!" I yelled and we picked up our stuff and ran for cover.

I can't imagine what the enemy observer must have thought as we sat still for three rounds while he corrected his hits closer and closer. "Those Marines are crazy!"

PT-76 Tank

A very light, amphibious Russian tank with a healthy 76mm main gun. I did not see one of these while I was in Vietnam, but I could imagine the shock and surprise of the Special Forces folks who did at Lang Vei. If you had a LAW rocket launcher and the presence of mind to aim it, the PT-76 would have been toast – but having that presence of mind is a rare thing.

T-54 Tank

The Russians somewhat crudely referred to this version of their T-54 as the "Monkey model," made for export to some of their more primitive allies and missed some of the more modern features, like rangefinders and fume evacuators on the barrel. Nonetheless, if one of these showed up, you'd have your hands full; since it was rugged and dependable, and heavily armored, with a very powerful 122mm gun and usually a 12.7mm heavy machinegun on top of the turret. Like their heavy artillery, the NVA kept these beauties near their main infiltration bases and we generally didn't run into them unless we went to them. Except for the improved roads which were few and far between, Vietnam was not "tank country."

Appendix 3

THIS IS THE LETTER THAT I PROVIDED TO THE WOUNDED MARINES and sailors that I visited at Bethesda Naval Hospital and Walter Reed Hospital during the height of the Iraq and Afghanistan Wars.

BEING WOUNDED

None of us really expects to get hit but when we are, there are a whole bunch of things that happen to us no matter how prepared we think we are. It's happening to you now: you are among the most recent of a long line of Marines that have been severely injured in combat. There are fellow Marines that have gone through their own version of this before you and if we could, we'd like to share some of our experiences to help you along with your recovery.

It hurts. No matter what you expected and unlike the movies, getting wounded carries serious pain with it. It's part of the body's defensive system but no matter what medication they give for you, pain is going to be your companion for a while. Pain is a very personal thing and it's something you'll have to take on all by yourself for a while. The only comfort I've got for you is that you have to be alive to feel the pain. Eventually, it will begin to ebb and hopefully go away.

Sometimes you'll feel guilty. It's a normal process in a tightly connected team like the Marine Corps to get feelings of regret that you survived where other Marines of yours did not or you may feel that you should still be there, supporting your unit. This is completely normal, and we all felt it. The important part to remember is that combat is combat: the whole purpose of combat is to kill and wound people and you got hit. It's not your fault and nobody, anywhere would think otherwise. Your getting hit may very well have saved someone else behind you. It's a little like being hit by lightning; and you were the one hit by the bolt and others were spared. Your primary duty to your unit and yourself now is to recover as completely as your body will allow.

You'll feel depression. This is also normal – this is a big change in your life, and it's filled with uncertainty and pain. The guilt feelings mentioned above or just the difficulties your recovery will face and accommodating a new future can cause depression to take hold. This is also normal and another obstacle to overcome. The best way to beat depression is to get close to your central values and your family. Your chaplain and your fellow Marines are dependable sources of comfort and if you need help dealing with depression, fight it through your faith and with the help of people near you. Talk about your situation with people you trust and get the issues off your chest. It's normal and expected and courageous to seek help.

People often don't react the way you thought they would. People are people. You'll get some odd questions about your experience because people are curious about what you've endured but they won't know how to express it properly. Sometimes people will say unthinking things and you'll have to be able to remember that they don't mean any harm and try to be the bigger person and answer with care. Others will try to ignore what has happened to you or avoid talking to you about any of your experiences. They may do this because they are trying to save you from having to relive your experience. They might also be trying to avoid discussing your involvement in combat when they have not served or have not been there and they feel guilty. The main thing you need to do is to comfort your loved ones and stay strong during this first hard part. It gets better later.

Dreams/"the flinches." Another part of recovery is the process of reliving some of your experiences in bad dreams and the other effect called the Startle Reaction or the "flinches." The dreams usually show up sometime within the first few months after combat and they are a result of your mind coming to grips with the extraordinary experiences you've had. Combat involves death and injury and other human shocks that no amount of training or preparation completely prepares you for. The dreams leave after a while after the mind acclimatizes to your new, safer situation and just remember that those dreams are completely normal for somebody who's gone through what you're going through. The "flinches" are also normal. You hear a loud noise – usually something that sounds like a shot – and you try to get under something or at least pull your head down into your neck. Happens to all of us and after a while, you'll quit doing that. Little brothers find this effect particularly funny.

Your life has changed. That's the main effect of being wounded; your life has changed by whatever remaining injury you'll have left after your recovery. How severely you were wounded controls a lot of that but there's also a component based on how strong you are within yourself. You control a lot of the progress and pace of your recovery by keeping your mind and your heart into it. How well you are able to get back to where you want to be again is to a great deal, something that you'll have to control. Redeveloping yourself takes strength and courage particularly if it will take overcoming some serious losses of your body. You will have to face those changes, overcome as much as you can overcome and become the new person that you are. There have been many thousands of us before you and most of us have done well with our new lives. Our thoughts and our prayers are with you in this new fight.

Remember one thing above all. You are now one of the few Marines that has bled for our team, our Corps, and our country. This price that you are paying and will pay has been for all of us, past, present, and future. No matter what you eventually achieve with your life, you will always know that you were one of the select few that has paid the price of being a Marine in combat. You will also know that you had the courage to take it and keep going. All of us who went before you, are proud of you and stand with you and we're here for you if you need us.

Semper Fi,

LtCol Forrest R. Lindsey, USMC (Ret.)
Wounded May 13, 1967